To Mick
from Ric
June, 08

Also by Richard Arthur DeRemee

Time and the Mystery of Consciousness

The Mick-Rick Debates:
Controversies in Contemporary Christianity
(with Michael Maasdorp)

Mick-Rick Essays on the Sacred & Profane
(with Michael Maasdorp)

ISBN: 1-4196-9326-3
ISBN-13: 9781419693267

Visit www.booksurge.com to order additional copies.

from a
SOLITARY ROOM

Stories and Essays

RICHARD ARTHUR DeREMEE

To the memories of Professors J. Luke Creel,
Gerhard T. Alexis and Robert Esbjornson

Who inspired my passion for writing
and the English Language

Contents

PART FIVE **Of Art and Artists**

PART SIX **Essays**

Preface

What does one do in retirement? It is a perennial question and a cliché. On March 31, 1996 I retired from the Mayo Clinic after serving more than 30 years as a physician. The next day I felt like a school boy having been released for summer vacation. The summers and all subsequent seasons of the years to come were now mine to use as I wished. Now I had my stipend so let the adventure begin. I could get up when I pleased, linger over my coffee with a couple of cigarettes (please don't bug me about that) and read the morning paper. If that isn't living, what is? Then, in the fullness of time, I would adjourn to my office, my solitary room to start to think and write.

My interest in writing began in childhood. I was given a flimsy wooden school desk by someone I don't remember. I recall sitting at the desk with paper and pencil trying to ply the new writing skills recently acquired in Hancock Elementary School. The simple books we read fascinated me. I thought how wonderful it must be to write books and have others read them. Perhaps I was on some kind of ego trip and my interest in books would facilitate a good outcome. Anyway, that's how it all began. These early efforts, I am sorry to say were not successful.

My literary urges lay dormant while I passed through elementary school. About the age of thirteen (maybe it coincided with puberty) there was a sudden burst of interest in the written word started by, of all things, a radio station. Some out-of-town entrepreneurs offered to establish a radio station if they could find support from the city government and investors. We had no radio station. Because we didn't, there were many, myself included, who thought Red Wing had not yet entered the modern age. I considered Red Wing to be backward and unexciting. I thought like the pubescent daughter who considers her parents uncool and doesn't want to be seen with them.

For many weeks following the proposal's announcement in the local paper, no further word was heard regarding the matter. I feared it had been withdrawn. Someone needed to act. There was too much inertia in town. We needed to pep things up.

Thus, I acted and wrote a letter to the editor of the Red Wing Republican Eagle. To my great surprise it was published! I saw my name in print for the first time! I was exhilarated.

The impetus was apparently not enough to carry me through high school so my writing again fell silent while I struggled with the tribulations of adolescence.

I matriculated at Gustavus Adolphus College in 1951. English 101 was taught by Gerhard T. Alexis. He was a short, proper, exacting, erudite, critical but fair, bow-tied task master. One of his early assignments was to write a brief story on a personal experience. Mine concerned duck hunting with an uncle.

He read selected stories aloud to make grammatical points. When he started reading mine a chill circled my scalp as I slouched down in my chair awaiting inevitable humiliation.

He read my piece without pause and with great dramatic emphasis I took for mocking. When he concluded he asked the class for their opinions. No one said a word. "That was one of the best stories I have ever read by one of my students." I was numb with surprise. The chill in my scalp grew more intense as I felt my face turning red with embarrassment. This was a seminal moment in the development of my literary career.

Subsequently I enrolled in a creative writing class taught by J. Luke Creel who had a very good reputation among the faculty literati. It was a marvelous time to hone my skills writing numerous stories, essays and poems. I published a number of stories and poems in the college literary magazine, *Prospects*.

In my senior year I wrote the text for our college annual. Professor Creel left me with a memorable aphorism. It should be your goal in life to make your avocation your vocation. He also introduced me to Ambrose Bierce.

Robert Esbjornson, a professor of religion and ethics, was to prove an inspiration for over 50 years until his death in 2007. Not only was he a great teacher but as well a prolific writer. As his specialty was medical ethics we were a perfect fit after I became a practicing physician. In later years he frequently came for overnights in my home in Rochester when we would enjoy wine and dinner and talk late into the night.

Following graduation I entered the Medical School of the University of Minnesota. This was an intense and demanding course that left me neither time nor motivation to write creatively. Immediately after medical school I enlisted in the U.S. Army serving three years in the Medical Corps. During this time I dabbled in poetry but produced little.

On discharge in 1962 I started specialty training at the Mayo Clinic. Now my writing took a different tack into the realm of science. My first scientific paper appeared in 1968. Over the next thirty plus years my bibliography would increase to more than 200 original articles, abstracts, editorials and letters all accomplished on top of my clinical duties.

Since retirement eleven years ago I have added over 40 more citations. These include a number of chapters in medical texts, more editorials, three books and a number of poems and stories.

Thus, I have finally followed Creel's admonition to make my avocation my vocation.

It is imperative for the writer to have some kind of sanctuary in which to retreat and think without distraction. For some this may be the out-of-doors in nature. For others it may be a café where the coffee and cigarette smoke are rich.

After my son, the youngest of three children left home, I con-fiscated his bedroom for my office. All his stuff was removed and replaced with custom-built office furniture. There are book shelves, cabinets, desk tops and a door that shuts off the ambient noises of the home. I have, of course, a computer and printer and a relic of the past called a FAX machine I still use from time to time. Some of my correspondents prefer to see my hand writing over my sterile renderings on E-mail. Thus, I am in touch with the world. It is in this solitary room I write.

PART ONE
From Youth And Family

A Rural Triptych

During World War II, I spent most of my summers on the farm of my Uncle Bill and Aunt Effie. Actually Bill was my great uncle being the brother of my maternal grandfather. He married Aunt Effie when they were both in their early 50's which probably accounts for their having no children. Before marriage, Effie was a country-school teacher. She and Bill had attended Gustavus Adolphus College where they first met. Why they hadn't married earlier was always a mystery to me. I never heard anyone discuss the matter. In any event it was a happy compatible union that enabled their magic farm to prosper.

They worked together very hard. The chief source of income was from the heavy cream their herd of Holstein cows produced and from which high quality butter was churned by the small local creamery in Vasa. The residual skim milk was fed either to new calves or mixed with ground grain for the immense grunting pigs. Most of the calves were sold for slaughter as were the pigs.

There were two milking sessions, 7AM and 6PM and of course this was seven days a week. On Sundays they might rush through the morning chores, go to church then drive a hundred miles to visit friends or relatives and return in time for the evening milking session. Only years later did I come to appreciate what baggage this must have been but they never complained. It was simply a way of life that had been good to them.

Bill and Effie joined forces to milk the cows, separate the cream, feed the animals and clean up all the paraphernalia entailed in the process. Cleanliness and above all sterility were of paramount importance in maintaining the quality and hence market value of the cream. It is hard to imagine how they maintained such high standards given the primitive methods used but they always were given the highest rating.

Between milkings, Effie cooked the meals, baked her prized Swedish rye bread, and did the house work. When the snow disappeared she was outside mowing the expansive lawn or tending the large flower and vegetable garden. Her diligence created environs as beautiful as anything I was ever to see in the finest gardens of Europe. Coming to the farm in high summer when all was lush green and the flowers were dancing in the breeze was always a treat to savor especially with a glass of lemonade or raspberry nectar prepared from her own raspberries.

The second source of income was from chickens, a large flock of Rhode Island reds usually managed by a huge rooster. The rooster of the day would occasionally lose his head to provide Sunday dinner and his successor would quickly take his place oblivious of the risk he was taking. The long line of ruling roosters bore similar characteristics of arrogance and authority that culminated in an incident that I will relate in due course. Effie was master of the hen house collecting the eggs, candling them and packing them in crates to be sent to market. I was her chief assistant, a task I enjoyed. It was fun to stick a hand under the warm bottom of a squawking hen to rob her of her efforts. A sudden noise or movement would cause a flurry of flapping wings that stirred a pungent cloud of dust. It was amazing we didn't get sick from all the dirt that must have entered our mouths and lungs during these frequent events.

The heavy physical work was done by Bill. The divisions of

labor were distinct with no arguments over what should be done or when it should be done. Their arrangements were a model for interpersonal relations. I can never recall an argument between this happy busy likeable pair. When their bodies could no longer manage the work they sold the farm and moved to a modest home in Red Wing where they spent their remaining years in the same happy mode. Bill died at age 90 a few months before Effie.

My thoughts return often to them and their farm which became a rich storehouse of memories and stories. Fortunately, before they left the farm I was able to take my three young children there to see them romp in Effie's park, taste the Sunday chicken, pick flowers and gingerly put their hands on the rough skin of the pigs. They were infused as I with the same sense of mysterious beauty this place held.

The farm is situated at the crossing of two gravel roads about one mile from the nearest blacktop. Following the blacktop road down a long hill called Lassa's Lee leads through a wooded valley connecting with U.S. highway 61 after about five miles. Taking a right on 61 shortly brings you to Red Wing, my home town. Although the distance from the farm to my home was only 12 miles the journey was immense in my pre-adolescent mind.

Vasa, the village with the creamery, was the center of activity for the farming community settled largely by first and second generation Swedish immigrants. It consisted of a few scattered houses, two general stores, and the creamery. On the hill dominating the landscape, arose like a whale breaking water, the spire of the Swedish Lutheran Church, the unifying symbol of the community. Built in the 1860's by the immigrants themselves, each brick was formed from local clay in fortunate abundance. The benches and other wood appointments were all fashioned from local hard woods by the skilled Swedish carpenters. There is a wainscot of tin around the nave that constitutes one of the few materials not natural to the area. After I first visited Sweden and its churches, I was struck by the faithful reproduction of Vasa Lutheran Church after its sisters in the home land.

The church provided a focus for the community economically, socially and spiritually. Here on Sundays the denizens shared their common problems and joys. Arrangements were made to help a sick colleague or to plan the route of the threshing machine for the upcoming harvest. When they died they were interred in the church yard just outside the main door. Many of my forebears rest there with a great view over the rolling plain. The church was the source of power that enabled them to endure the hardships required first by their poverty in Sweden then by the long journey to the Promised Land. Most survived the ordeal to prosper. With the perspective of time it is apparent that as a group they were girded by their faith with the kind of resilience necessary for their accomplishments in the new world. What was equally important, they constituted an extraordinary gene pool rife with intelligence, ambition and creativity.

Bill was just over six feet tall of sinewy construction, the kind one would expect of a man whose body was the engine of his occupation. His face was notable for heavy dark eyebrows that balanced a dense but neat squarely-trimmed moustache. Of course he had a farmer tan ending at his neck and elbows that was very funny to observe when he was naked in the basement ready for his shower. Good jokes and humor was his staple consistent with his temperament of basic happiness and a high sense of self-worth. He did have a temper that occasionally blazed, especially at an animal that did not obey. Then his mouth would curl into Swedish swear words, never English, curiously. One of his trademarks was the constant hand-rolled cigarette in his mouth from the moment he left the house. He rolled his next while the stub of the previous threatened to burn his lips. Then he would deftly remove it to fire the next specimen. I even saw him in the hay loft pitching hay while smoking. It is truly remarkable he never started a fire. One situation in which he never smoked while outside was in the straw stack built by the threshing machine. The spout poured out torrents of yellow straw over him as he attempted to distribute the material so as to stabilize the stack, building it into a perfect golden dome. Perhaps he was too busy with his hands or the stream of air was too fierce to allow a cigarette to flourish.

Another place he never smoked was in the house except for the basement. It is not clear how this smoking arrangement came about so long before tobacco was generally considered to be a health hazard and before the current severe restrictions of smoking in public places. Agreements must have been made of mutual satisfaction for never did I hear Effie say anything about Bill's smoking. He continued to smoke until shortly before his death. I wonder if he ever considered cutting down or even stopping for health reasons. Perhaps if he had, he might have exceeded 90 years. I'll wager he would not have bartered his cigarettes for a few extra days or months.

In retrospect, proscription of smoking upstairs was a gift to me because it created a ritual of great fascination. Whenever company came for dinner, it was the custom for the smokers (they were all men) to adjourn to the basement to light up "tailor-mades" as they were called. These were readymade cigarettes from packages. In Bill's case these were Raleigh's with cork tips but no filter. I was always invited to attend these soirees although, of course, I did not smoke. To this day the smell of a freshly-lit cigarette conjures the fascination of those interesting moments.

Effie had snow white hair all her life, a genetic trait reflected in her brother and father. She kept her hair in neat tight curls protected each night with a net. Her voice was high in pitch with a pleasing cheerful timbre. The many years of physical work shaped her trim figure which moved with vigor and determination. I doubt there was ever a time she was unsure of what to do next. I suspect I was their surrogate grandchild for that is how I was treated. They seemed happy to see me come but my departures at the end of the summer were never contested. They were a couple that did not need children for their fulfillment. A little tangential contact with the young was sufficient.

Among other smells having importance to me are the aromas of Effie's Sunday chicken, rye bread, and Sunday waffles with strawberries and whipped cream. How in the world did these two achieve such longevity with all the rich food they ate? The Sunday waffles topped with thick whip cream in which fresh strawberries were folded was such a favorite of mine. To this day waffles have been an unfailing tradition in my home. The whip cream and strawberries are for ultra-special occasions.

Even though rye bread was a daily element of every meal it was always welcome. In particular I recall its excellence for sandwiches. When field work was at its height, Effie would pack a lunch in a large wicker basket that she and I carried to Bill wherever he was engaged. The sandwiches usually contained meat such as dried beef or ham generously spread with butter, no margarine even though it was war time and butter was rationed. They of course could churn their own butter. It was a sin to use margarine in their view. The beverage was coffee containing sugar and cream. Even on hot sweaty August afternoons it was a perfect complement to those hearty sandwiches. Desert usually consisted of one or two home baked cookies then back on the tractor. Those lunches in the field initiated my taste for coffee even though I was just over age ten. When I smell it I can close my eyes to see high stands of corn, freshly mowed alfalfa or newly harvested fields of wheat and oats.

During those wonderful rural summers my clothes consisted primarily of bib overalls, short sleeved shirts, high top leather work boots and a broad-brimmed straw hat. Straw hats are great protectors from the sun. When the head gets too hot, douse the hat in water and put it back on. A straw hat redolent with sweat triggers sweet memories. My ensemble was perfect for my work.

In addition to mowing the lawn and picking eggs with Effie, I usually helped with the milking chores. I became fairly proficient in stripping the cows after the milking machine was removed. For those not familiar with the farm and in particular dairy farming, stripping is the manual extraction of the last few ounces of milk that usually remain after mechanical milking. It develops great hand-finger strength. Bill had hand-milked for some thirty years before he got milk machines. This activity left him with odd deformities of the thumbs cause by the repetitive pressure on the cow's teats.

I also carried pails of milk to the cream separator, and took the skim to the impatient calf or to the grunting pigs. When morning cleanup was done Effie headed for the kitchen while Bill and I took the heavy cream cans to the pump house for cooling. The pump house was built of concrete blocks containing an electric pump and water pressure system. Before the pump house was established, water had to be pumped from a well either by hand or by wind mill. Rural electrification brought a significant advance. As well as the water pressure system the pump house contained a deep cistern filled with cold water into which we lowered the cream cans. During his entire career Bill relied on this method for cooling. In spite of this relatively primitive method he never sustained a decrease in the quality of his cream. The pump house was a friendly place to retire in the heat for a cold scoop of water from a tin cup. It was also to be the site of a very important event to be related later.

Following morning chores, breakfast was served in the kitchen usually starting with dry cereal. During the war, rationing greatly restricted the use of sugar so we were accustomed to using corn syrup on our cereal. Bill began to use saccharin tablets in his coffee. I note that the bottle had written on it "soluble" which I pronounced "suh <u>luhb</u> l". Somehow this tickled Bill who reminded me of my funny verbal *faux pas* up to the time he died.

Cereal was followed by the inevitable fried eggs usually over easy, accompanied either by ham or bacon. Bill had a curious way of eating eggs. First he would eat all the white and then pop the yolk in his mouth with a gulp. I never really understood this ritual. All was consumed with slices of rye toast laced with butter. Given today's concern over fat and cholesterol I shudder to think how we were unknowingly killing ourselves. It sure tasted good and set us up for the work ahead.

The huge lawn was mowed weekly usually taking just over one day to complete if Effie was working alone. My help reduced the time to a full morning and a short afternoon so my contribution was significant and fully recognized. Behind our push reel mowers were grass catchers that we emptied on ever growing piles at the edge of the garden to be used for mulch. Some of the clippings were scattered near the hen house to be pecked up by the busy brown hens while the giant rooster raised his head above his harem, spying out danger.

An Unlucky Rabbit

In addition to the jobs already mentioned I was assigned the role of pest controller. This included trapping moles and gophers as well as shooting rabbits. The latter were particularly bothersome taking a large toll on Effie's vegetables. Thus, the efficiency of my efforts was of major interest to her. Moles and gophers seemed so soulless that it was not a major moral crisis for me to dispose of them. Rabbits were a different matter as they had long soft ears and reminded me of children's toys. Also, I could not ignore the possibility that one could be the Easter bunny. But, I steeled myself and went out to do my job if with some reluctance.

I did not use a gun to shoot rabbits. Rather, a sling shot was my lethal weapon. This I made myself from the crotch of a tree branch and rubber from a discarded inner tube. Without bragging too much I must say I became an excellent shot, at times bringing down my prey from considerable distances. In between hunts my skills were honed on targets on the side of the barn. My ammunition was selected from a gravel road with size and shape of the projectiles being crucial to the range I was to shoot.

One summer I dispatched over 20 rabbits. My most remarkable shot occurred shortly after lunch one hot late July afternoon. I had just left the house to go to the barn while Bill took his regular post-prandial half hour nap. Just as I passed the giant maple tree half way to the barn a huge rabbit poked his twitching nose from under a hedgerow 50 yards away. In typical rabbit fashion he froze while he assessed the danger. (My reputation must have been known to the entire rabbit community. What did they call me? I fancied.) Moving slowly I simultaneously reached for my weapon hanging from my left rear pocket while my right hand searched a front pocket for a stone. In slow motion I engaged the missile in the leather sling drawing the rubber bands back while my left hand steadied the wooden Y. By that time my experience had programmed me well for trajectory and prevailing wind. As I was about to release, the rabbit darted back into a gap in the hedge obscuring him from view. Without a conscious thought my automatic fire control made the appropriate corrections to send the stone flying precisely to the imagined position of my target under the hedge. It was a perfect shot I thought.

With a whoop I leaped to evaluate the result. Crouching down to peer under the hedge I was unexpectedly caught up by a sense of pity and shame I had not previously experienced. Quite dead the rabbit was lying on his right side, eyes wide open. The projectile struck him cleanly on the head and lay just under his nose with a spot of blood on it. It must have been a quick painless death I told myself. What an incredible shot, unbelievable and a blind one at that. How could I have done it?

No matter how much I tried to savor the excellence of my marksmanship, I did not feel good about myself. This was a different kill. Most of the others had been caught red handed in the garden committing their crimes. Their punishment seemed appropriate and they usually had their eyes closed when I picked them up to bury them. This rabbit was different. He was not raiding the garden. Perhaps he had in the past or maybe he never did, being content to eat the wild grasses and leaves. And he seemed to be just coming out of the hedge to catch some warm sun or a cool breeze. Then I appeared. I was a killer, an avenger of the garden. My lucky shot was his misfortune. But this was only a nuisance rabbit. Why should I feel so deeply?

My rabbit hunting ceased after this experience. Fortunately I was about to return home so my continuation as rabbit slayer was interrupted by circumstance and not entirely by my newly found moral revulsion. Bill sensed a change in my feelings about rabbits, I could tell but he never asked me about it. There were still more summers on the farm to come but I never returned to rabbit hunting.

The Terrible Rooster

On July 4, 1943 I celebrated my tenth birthday. Shortly thereafter I went to the farm for the remainder of the summer. As my mother turned the car into the graveled drive to the farm the sight of the large square house and the red barn made my heart pound with excitement. When the car stopped I bounded out, running toward the barn to inspect my old haunts. All the smells filled me with memories of other exciting summers. Strange as it may seem, the smell of animal manure was particularly poignant. To this day such smells immediately conjure visions of the farm.

I first went to see old Pete, the giant bull who stood patiently in his confining pen waiting patiently for his next assignment. Next I paid my respects to my old friends King and Queen, the magnificent huge draft horses who still worked pulling wagons. They were undoubtedly relieved by the advent of the tractor for plowing. Finally, after inspecting the hogs, I jumped up to the flat roof that joined the main barn to the hog house. There, I had previously sat many evenings to watch the sun set. I could see for many miles over the undulating countryside while the colors changed from orange to red, then to purple while the fields went to sleep.

After satisfying myself that my kingdom was in order I ran back to the house where mom and Effie were drinking coffee and eating Swedish sugar cookies. "Hi, Dickie," Effie smiled in her high pleasant voice. "It's great to have you back. Bill needs your help more than ever. It's going to be a busy summer for you." I was delighted to be needed.

That summer Effie's 94 year old mother took up residence in a downstairs room that was specially outfitted. She was too frail to climb stairs but if the weather was fair she took short walks in the farm yard. After a few halting steps braced by her cane she would have enough and with my help return to her room for a nap. She always wore a scarf over her head not only for warmth but to hide her almost complete baldness. A black cardigan sweater covering a print dress guarded by a snow white kitchen apron constituted her daily attire. The apron was a residual symbol of her former role as a Swedish farm wife. Her speech was halting, her facial expressions stony. During my medical studies I became aware that all her symptoms conformed to the diagnosis of Parkinson's disease. That winter grandma would die and confidently join her husband in heaven where he had gone thirty years before her. In the meantime she and I would be participants in a drama.

I have previously called attention to the rooster who managed the large flock of hens. By a process of natural selection each year one male would succeed in conquering all contenders to become the absolute monarch. It was remarkable how big they grew. This summer's King was a least three feet from the ground to the top of his erect pink comb. Being a Rhode Island Red his basic color was a dark reddish brown that turned into a copper sheen rising in his neck. He strode with broad, jerky steps, his head held high turning to all sides like a radar antenna looking for any threats to his concubines. He was intimidating not only due of his awesome physical appearance but also for his tiger-like temperament.

That blazing hot August afternoon grandma had just started her jerky stroll as I was leaving for the barn. The rooster stood amongst his hens about thirty yards away. The hens bobbed up and down pecking the ground while the rooster was suddenly still. I could tell he was drawing a bead on grandma. Dropping his head he slowly made his way between the indifferent hens, his eyes fixed on his target. Then he broke into a bounding run and with a giant flapping leap landed on grandma's head. He pecked her as she tried to defend herself but her aged arms were ineffective. Transfixed, I stood about fifty yards away observing the despicable attack. The event so shocked me I did not immediately think to act. Fortunately Effie had heard her mother's furtive cry for help and came running to the rescue brushing the bird away with a few sturdy swipes. After the reproach the rooster stood off a few yards and then bounded off as Effie ran after him waving her arms. "That nasty bird…are you alright, mother?" "Yes, yes," the old lady said in her monotone voice. "What's gone wrong with that bird?" grandma said as she returned to her quarters. It would be some time before she ventured out. She was truly afraid of the terrible rooster.

For two weeks or more a reign of terror ensued. Grandma would not go out. I became the next victim. Each time I started out alone for the barn he chased me with bounding step and blazing eyes. I was usually able run to a shelter of sorts but it was always a close race as he pecked at my heels. The sunset-watching roof was a frequent refuge. There I would wait until the red devil lost interest in me and strutted off to attend his waiting darlings. This was crazy. What had happened to the bird? I was at once angry and fascinated. He was acting like a jealous husband or more like the town bully.

Bill found it all very amusing. He appeared to enjoy the spectacle of a ten year old boy running for his life, with a big rooster in hot pursuit. The rooster never attacked Bill or Effie so they became my body guards going to the barn.

As I tried to fall asleep those sticky summer nights I could think of nothing but that rooster. I became more and more angry. He was destroying my life. I've got to do something about it. He attacked the infirm and the young but not the strong. He was the classic bully. He had to be brought down. Night after night these thoughts kept me from falling quickly to sleep. It took many such nights to galvanize my courage. One Friday morning I awoke with resolve to conquer my nemesis.

I fashioned a four foot willow branch for my weapon. Over and over I said to myself, you've got to do it, today's the day, you've got to be brave or he'll always have you on the run.

After breakfast, while Effie was clearing the breakfast dishes and Bill was in the basement workshop making some repairs, I slipped out the back door and grasped the willow I had placed nearby. A hundred yards away the head of my opponent rose above the brown sea of hens like the loch Ness monster breaching the surface. He saw me coming. It was my plan to pretend I was going out to the pump house, not to the barn, so as to decoy him near a possible refuge if I should be defeated. Undoubtedly he would rush me but I would be ready.

My heart was bounding, my throat dry, I was shaking almost ready to abort my plan. After all, why should a bird be such a problem to me? He'll be in Effie's roaster before long. Why don't I forget this silly combat? My courage began to waver. Then I said to myself, next summer there'll be another one who will probably do the same thing and I must face up to them all.

Courage of the mind is different than that of the spirit. The former depends on a conscious rational internal discourse to find its reason for being. Courage of the spirit is instinctual beyond the rational. It is displayed in physical combat particularly in war time when soldiers win medals for performing heroic acts or in selfless sacrifice for a comrade. It is done without conscious thought; it wells up from the deep subconscious, a product of the complex process of growing up in a certain environment.

I had no time for extended thought. From my peripheral vision I could see him bearing down on me, head low, wings extended as if he were about to take off. Courage of the spirit switched on. I waited, looking at right angles to his trajectory. Just as he sprang into the air for attack I turned abruptly swinging my willow. I was angry, not afraid. The willow caught him squarely on his left side sending him rolling to the ground where he lay transiently immobilized. I stood over the stunned bird shouting at him, "You won't scare me or anyone else anymore". He had met his match. Timidly he arose to his haunches, then to full height slinking off to the comfort of his flock. I couldn't let him off this easy, recounting all the injury he had caused. My anger did not subside.

I ran after him swinging my willow. Squawking, he ran back and forth; finally he made a break for the pump house I had held in reserve for my own escape. He was fast. I could barely keep up with him in my pursuit as he bounded in the door to the dark interior. The sun was bright so it took some time to adapt my vision to the darkness. I could not see him. There were a number of potential hiding places, behind pails, behind pipes, behind the door. The rooster didn't make a sound.

Cautiously I reached my hand around the door casement to find the light switch. For a moment, as my anger began to cool, I thought of the possibility of a counterattack out of the darkness; that made me wary. I flicked the switch. There, huddled behind a three gallon pail was my once proud antagonist, head low, eyes darting in fright. I continued the humiliation methodically. A long handled drinking ladle hung on the wall nearby. Repeatedly I filled it with water and then slowly poured over the frightened chicken. Again and again I poured as if to leach the pride and ferocity from him. It was long enough to cool my anger. Then as I sat on the cool concrete floor, the ladle drooping from my hand a sudden remorse and pity came over me as I watched the huddled rooster, no longer three feet tall, no longer proud and fierce. All my passion had subsided as the rooster slinked along the wall to the open door from which he blasted like a jet plane on takeoff. He ran in giant steps back to his hens; they surprisingly paid him no particular attention. Soon he returned to his usual head high demeanor but a change had occurred. No longer was he a threat to anyone. Grandma resumed her walks without fear. I went freely about the farm yard. Whenever I came near the rooster he sauntered off to busy himself with something on the ground.

For fifty years this experience has remained fresh and palpable. Since that August afternoon a number of roosters have crossed my path trying to intimidate me or others. Some of them ended up as did the terrible rooster.

Threshing Day

The greatest event on the farm was threshing day. It is hard to appreciate this event at a time when grain is harvested by solitary combines. Threshing day was one of the busiest, intense days of the year in addition to being a prime social occasion. The story I am about to tell is based on the composite experiences of the summers of 1943 and 1944.

First you must understand what a threshing machine is. Essentially it is a huge sheet metal box about 30 feet long, 12 feet high and six feet wide. It strides on four large, spooked metal wheels, the front two being steerable. The front of the machine has a large mouth-like opening with a conveyor belt that receives the grain bundles and carries them to the gnashing, gyrating teeth that tear the bundles open after which they are swallowed into the bowels of the machine where, by a mysterious noisy process, they are separated into grain and straw. (The term "separator" is used interchangeably with threshing machine). A metal spout about twenty feet in length and one foot in diameter protrudes from the opposite end of the machine and discharges the straw. The separated grain is neatly dispensed by a tube with a screw into a measuring device that counts and records in units of bushels. As there is a limited storage capacity within the machine, it is necessary to periodically unload grain into container vehicles for transport to the granary. If I squinted, I could see a dragon.

Because the straw stack gradually builds up, progressive angulations of the spout are required. Stacks often reach heights of 30 or more feet. In order to prevent the stack from collapsing and spreading out, someone must stand at its pinnacle to properly distribute the straw. The one selected for this dirty, hot work was usually the host farmer if he was physically up to the job.

Grain shocks were brought from the field to the separator on bundle wagons drawn by two horses. The wagons were low and broad with fence-like barriers on the front and back. The sides were open enabling easy loading. One man pitched the bundles from the tented shocks while a second arranged them in stable layers up to the height of the barriers. Then the cargo was driven back alongside the noisy separator to be pitched into its noisy mouth. A number of bundle wagons were active in various stages of loading and unloading, coming and going. The air was shimmering with intense sounds, the roar of the separator, the coarse hum of the tractor powering the machine, the whoosh of the straw, the clink of the measuring device, men yelling at horses and the horses responding with high pitched whinnying. It was a great cacophony which required shouting to be heard.

When riding a bundle wagon I was fascinated by the receding sound as we drove out to the field to fetch another load. When reloaded, coming back toward the separator the sound level would gradually swell in a crescendo. It was like standing on a street corner watching a parade, and hearing the sound of the bands growing then retreating in the distance.

In 1944, at age eleven I had reached sufficient physical maturity to serve on a bundle wagon to arrange bundles and drive the horses thus providing a useful service.

The players in this exciting production were farmers of the small community of Vasa. The separator was owned by one of the more well-to-do farmers who rented it by the hour. Since the harvest window was about two weeks and each farmer's crop took one full day, only 14 clients could be served in a season by one separator. All the participant farmers teamed up to help each other. Usually each brought with him a hired man so that the total work force was in the neighborhood of 30 at each threshing event.

All the men in Bill's group were first or second generation immigrant Swedes. Swedish was the language of choice in the fields particularly when cursing or admonishing the horses. The sing song lilt of Swedish seemed a proper accompaniment to the pastoral scene.

My excited anticipation of threshing day was equal to that of Christmas. Bill, Effie and I would hurry through the morning milking chores and then through the usual substantial breakfast. Then out to the barn to hitch up the horses and mobilize the tractor. Next I would rush to the edge of the road. There I listened for the crunching sound of the separator, the clop and clang of the horse-drawn wagons, and the chug of the tractors as they arose in the distance like an army on the march. A billow of dust could be seen where the symphony of sounds emanated, next the sing song Swedish, then the full-blown armada face to face. At that time in life I had not yet gained the images of Rome. Today, when I listen to Respighi's Pines of Rome, particularly when the Roman Legions are marching on the Apian Way, I can visualize the magnificent procession of the separator grinding ever closer with its entourage of hearty Swedish farmers in their horse-drawn wagons. It was electrifying. Nothing in my subsequent experience has aroused more excitement in me than did this remarkable pageant of my youth.

Suddenly the previously quiet farm yard was alive with activity. The separator was drawn into position in an open field near the barn. The tractor, an old green Oliver that pulled the separator, disengaged and maneuvered into position to power the separator. Power was supplied by a long belt strung from the tractor power take off to a wheel on the separator.

The alignment had to be perfect or the belt would slip off. To achieve proper alignment in the first try was a cause for congratulations to the skillful engineer.

After the belt was attached, the signal was given to engage the power. A few snorts issued from the straining tractor. Slowly at first, then with increasing speed the great belt turned on its pulleys. The separator began with a low whir which changed to an increasingly high pitched whine as full power was reached. Next, ancillary gears, belts, and axles were engaged resulting in a cacophony of sound making me quiver with excitement.

Back in the barn yard a veritable traffic jam ensued as wagons of various type awaited clearance to proceed to their appointed tasks; the bundle wagons to the field, the grain wagons back and forth from the granary.

At precisely 12 o'clock noon all activity ceased. The separator whirred down to silence. The wagons with their teams returned to the shade of the farm yard. Lunch was served. Before eating, the farmers went to the stock watering tank to dunk their hats and heads in the cool water. They would then shake, like wet dogs to remove the water. No soap was needed.

Effie's rye bread sandwiches and sugar cookies were liberally distributed to the hungry men sitting on the grass, their straw hats now at their sides exposing farmer tans. A short while ago these men who worked with great vigor and determination now were in perfect high noon repose in the shade eating a country banquet. After eating, a few would lie back, place their straw hat over the face, and put their hands behind their head and fall fast asleep. Some even snored. The air was rife with coffee and cardamom encircling and filtering between the sing song Swedish. The scene was a montage of sights, sounds, smells and textures. I was enthralled.

By late afternoon all was finished. The bundles had been

cleared from the fields leaving them with the look of newly shorn sheep. The straw stack had reached almost 40 feet. It had a symmetric rounded dome giving the appearance of a Roman basilica in the late afternoon sun. The grain was safe in the granary overflowing with the excellent crop. Down the road the brooding separator sauntered off to its next assignment. It seemed to be pleased with its performance. Gradually the farmers bid their Swedish good byes as they hurried home for the evening chores.

I was terribly let down. How could I possibly endure the long year until the dragon and his happy crew returned for another threshing day? That night, sleep came rapidly as I tried to recount the fabulous day.

The Pitcher and the Bat Boy

I smoked my first cigarette in the summer of 1951 at the age of eighteen. Graduation from high school had occurred a few weeks before. All during high school I was involved in athletics including football, basketball and baseball the latter being my favorite and in which I did well as a pitcher. In those days it was taboo for athletes to smoke so I never gave much thought to it or was ever tempted. It is an irony of sorts that baseball led to my smoking habit.

One of my best friends was also my catcher. He had smoked openly throughout high school to the amazement of none especially his mother. I'm not sure when he started smoking but I vaguely recall watching him light up one of his mother's Philip Morris one autumn Saturday afternoon as we listened to the Minnesota football game and charted the plays. His mother was in town shopping. We were in our early teens.

My friend's mother was a very sophisticated and nice lady. I liked her very much. In a way she was a sort of female role model for me. She had studied at the *Sorbonne* in Paris and naturally spoke fluent French. That was quite something for anyone in Red Wing. Periodically she returned to France, particularly in the fall to visit old friends. I loved to hear her talk about France, especially Paris. When she spoke in French- that I coaxed her to do on many occasions- I would close my eyes and paint mind pictures of what I thought it would be like to be there. In fact, I think she played a large role in fostering my interest in foreign languages and travel; I am grateful for that. Here was this fantastic woman who spoke French and who traveled the world. She should have been living in New York, not Red Wing.

Her gifted upbringing was well known to the people in Red Wing. Yet, she fit in. Never did I sense any arrogance or condescension nor did she ever flaunt her French in public. She loved to smoke and have cocktails before dinner.

The story goes that her parents sent her to France in the late 1920's in the hopes of breaking up a relationship she had with a young man of whom they disapproved. Four whole years she remained in Paris but promptly on return to Red Wing married him. It is still amazing to me how the relationship could have been maintained over such time and distance. The marriage produced two sons. The older became a successful farmer. The younger was nicknamed Skip and was my dear friend, battery mate and cigarette smoker.

Those not knowledgeable about baseball will have difficulty appreciating the importance of a catcher to a pitcher. He is the governor, the strategist, psychiatrist and cheerleader all in one. Skip and I fit together perfectly. Never was I to meet anyone who was more effective in bringing out my best efforts nor anyone more consoling in defeat. From the tenth grade to the end of high school we collaborated in a long succession of baseball triumphs. I don't exactly recall how many low hit games I pitched but there were quite a few. None would have been possible without my steady friend behind the plate.

In addition to triumphs there were defeats. One in particular was most agonizing. In the summer of 1950 we had an exceptional team, solid at every position. We were one game from qualifying for the state American Legion championship tournament. It was a night game in the opponent's town. As might be expected the crowd was partisan. Only a few of our best fans drove the hundred miles to cheer us on. Skip's mom was there. The opposing team also had a good pitcher and we became locked in a so-called pitcher's duel.

Our age level dictated only seven inning games. As we came to bat in the top of the seventh the score was tied at zero. I had pitched a two hitter to that point and I felt strong and confident. It was exhilarating to feel so good so far into the game. I could have gone ten innings I thought. My fast ball was still alive and popping into Skip's mitt. My breaking ball was falling off the table as connoisseurs would say.

The other pitcher was also quite effective. I don't recall how many hits he had allowed but he was tough with men on base and in spite of a few close calls he had given up no runs. We were the visiting team having first at bats in the seventh, the last regular inning. Our poorest hitters were set down in order. Skip hollered encouragement as I strode confidently to the mound for the bottom of the seventh. Surely we would retire them with dispatch to allow our best hitters to win it in extra innings.

Then the cruelest incident of my entire baseball career occurred. The opposing manager sent the bat boy to the plate to start the inning. Most boys of age 16 have nearly attained adult height. I was six feet though I weighed only 150 pounds. Thus, I was accustomed to pitching to a fairly generous strike zone. I had been piercing it with devilish speed and accuracy until the bat boy stepped up. At most he was four feet tall. When he crouched at the plate he presented a strike zone that was as small as a silver dollar. Our manager vehemently complained to the umpire but to no avail since the diminutive culprit was duly entered in the pre-game roster. He was eligible to play.

The kid never took the bat off his shoulder as I'm sure his manager instructed him. I sent my first fast ball blazing over the plate but at the level of the kid's ears. Ball one! Skip motioned calmly to get the next pitch down and fired the ball back to me. For the first time in the game I began to feel unsure. I kicked my leg high and bounced the next pitch off the plate, the kid cowered unaware the ball had passed. Ball two!

Skip called time and ran to the mound for a conference. "Come on big boy, don't worry, we'll get him. Even if we don't we'll take care of it." I could smell the smoke on Skip's breath as we huddled. His words bolstered my confidence but not my accuracy. I was aiming the ball not throwing it. All pitchers know what that means. Walking behind the mound I grabbed the rosin bag, gave a few puffs to my pitching hand and returned to work. Ball three! Ball four! I simply could not find that silver dollar strike zone. In spite of the predicament I was in, a fleeting admiration for the crafty manager crossed my mind. His strategy had worked.

Our manager called another conference at the mound. Skip and the infielders gathered around me as we planned our countermeasures. The kid was slow so a double play setup seemed appropriate. If he tried to steal second, Skip's rifle arm would do him in.

The conference ended. I put my right foot on the rubber and went into my stretch to hold the runner who had taken a puny lead at first. As I threw to the plate the kid broke for second as if in slow motion. Skip took the pitch, jumped to his feet as he snapped off his mask and began jumping toward the mound while faking throws to first then second. The runner did not flinch. It became quickly apparent the bat boy was on a mission not to be deterred. When the runner was half way to second base Skip unleashed a mighty throw to the shortstop covering the bag for the easy tag.

If I close my eyes I can still see the ball soaring over the shortstop's head into center field. Maybe it was sweat from my hands that made the ball slippery. Maybe it was something more profound and fateful that caused the ball to go amiss. The center fielder backing up the play hurried in as the runner rounded second on his way to third as his manager urged him on with flailing arms.

There was heavy dew on that late evening ball field. Drawing up to retrieve the ball the centerfielder's legs went out from under him and he lay on his back looking at the stars and a sliver of the moon. By the time the surprised left fielder had recovered the ball and fired it home it was too late. The game was over.

While our opponents shouted and danced in victory we slouched in shock in the locker room. I broke down, my body shaking in sobs over the agony of that moment. The whole world seemed empty. Skip came to me in his sweat-soaked under shirt. "It was my fault, I'm awful sorry." Strangely, I regained my composure. Suddenly I had the feeling none of us were to blame. We were good. We had prepared well. The story that had played out seemed too well designed and scripted to be an accident. We were just the actors carrying out our roles. It was perfect. Still it was at least a transient agony. Though a cigarette might have tasted good at that time I was still not a smoker.

After high school Skip and I went to different colleges but for two successive summers we renewed our collaboration on the baseball diamond competing in summer leagues. It was to be our final chapter. After one game he offered me a Philip Morris. I took it.

Skip did not do well in college because as his mother said, "He did not apply himself." When the Korean War came along he was drafted and served as a tank driver in that curious war. He was involved in a number of fierce battles and as he said, "I was frequently near death but never wounded." The war experience was transforming. After discharge from the army he enrolled in law school. He achieved a sparkling record graduating with distinction into a very prestigious law firm. He thus joined the profession of his long deceased father.

While I was in my residency training in internal medicine, Skip and his wife came to visit. We were in our early 30's. I had three children. He had one, a son, Bill. Skip had just finished a medical examination at my institution. With amazing calm he told me he was dying of cancer, not of the lung but of the colon.

He's been gone over thirty years. I saw his wife just once since his death but I never met his son. I should try and look him up some day

From time to time as I light up a cigarette and take a deep drag I am reminded of Skip. I see the ball soaring over the shortstop's head while the bat boy speeds for home. That event has long since lost its emotional edge. The pungent smell of cigarette smoke continues to evoke the drama and mystery of that momentous game and my buddy with smoke on his breath.

Rendezvous

In my early teens I had a great friend, Fred. Because he was tall and gangly, I nicknamed him "Slats." Eventually the name changed to "Schlitz" given the similarity of sound and his affinity for the beer of the same name. Fifty years later he happily responds to the same nickname his good friends continue to use.

Before girlfriends got in the way we were inseparable, particularly during the summer when we cruised in his family's old Pontiac sedan. In Red Wing there was always a friendly bunch to hang out with. They were pretty tame compared with today. We drank the odd beer but it never led to any trouble.

Duck hunting was one of our favorite shared interests. In late summer we enjoyed exploring potential hunting spots using my uncle's aluminum boat with a five horse motor. This was called "scouting ducks." Obviously, what ducks we saw were unlikely to remain until we arrived with our guns many weeks later. It was still called "scouting ducks." On these scouting trips we might take a few beers with us to slake our thirst from the heat.

Our favorite place to go scouting and hunting was Spring Creek Lake. The lake is more of a swamp than a lake. It is filled with bull rushes interspersed with patches of open water that attracts weary ducks on their migration southward. In the dense bull rushes we could create a blind to cover ourselves and the boat from the wary eyes of the duck. A good blind was essential for success.

To reach Spring Creek Lake requires a three to four mile boat ride from the Red Wing boat harbor. The first mile is upstream on the Mississippi to the entry of the smaller Cannon River. The Cannon is a narrow faster stream. It arises in south central Minnesota in farm country and then meanders through hardwood forest, between bluffs and finally through marshland before joining the Mississippi. Spring Creek Lake is a part of the terminal marsh. The Cannon is a remnant of the glacier that covered Minnesota 35,000 years ago. At the time of hunting season, current on the Mississippi is about 5 miles per hour in contrast to the Cannon which may exceed ten miles per hour. For motor boats these currents pose no significant impediment. For two teenage hunters in Schlitz's heavy old wooden row boat the currents were a serious factor in planning.

The duck season usually opens in early October. Cold wind and clouds are ideal to keep the ducks moving increasing the chances they will cross the sights of our guns. In Minnesota, October can be unpredictable. There can be ideal hunting weather or clear, warm days reminiscent of late summer. Under those conditions the ducks are either flying high out of range or lazing about on quiet ponds thus reducing their exposure to the gun.

The disadvantage to the duck hunter is that he is stationary in the blind depending on the duck to come to him. This contrasts with the pheasant or grouse hunter who seeks out his prey often with the aid of a dog who can flush the birds. The duck hunter is passive except for the process of getting to the hunting site. Dogs can be used to fetch downed ducks but they play no role in attracting or discovering them. We had no dog.

One autumn, Schlitz and I spent weeks planning for opening day. Our first consideration was timing. Shooting started one half hour before sunrise. At 44 degrees north latitude sunrise occurs at about seven o'clock in early October. Working backward we wanted to be in the blind and ready for action by six thirty. The position we scouted out in late summer would take at least two hours to reach with hard rowing. That meant departing the boat harbor no later than four thirty. Getting organized and driving to the harbor would take a half hour. We would need another half hour for a good breakfast to fuel our heavy efforts. Thus, we calculated a wake up time of three o'clock would provide an ample buffer.

That night I slept at Schlitz's house. We had our gear packed by ten o'clock. His little brother sulked as we finished our preparations. He was too young and too little to endure the anticipated rigors of our expedition. Anyway, who would want a little brother with? The degree of his apparent resentment gave us some concern he might sabotage our plans. This proved baseless, at least this time.

Typical of teenage boys, we crashed into sleep on hitting the bed. The alarm was set for two o'clock so we would have a good four hours of sleep. It seemed only minutes before we were aroused by the tinny sound of the windup alarm clock. With excitement we bounded out of bed and within minutes we were in the Pontiac heading for the river. The streets were deserted.

The night was cool, not cold. The stars shown brightly in a cloudless sky. It was not the kind of weather we had hoped for. We needed wind and clouds. Maybe the weather would change. As we ate our bacon and eggs in the all-night diner the cook commented that the weather forecast was for a clear day. "It should be great for you guys to be outside on such a nice day." He obviously was not a duck hunter. Schlitz and I glanced at each other. I could see the concern in his face.

On reaching the harbor we saw no one. The sky was still cloudless. Quickly we transferred our gear to the old row boat deployed earlier in the day. Schlitz took the first turn on the oars digging deeply in the black water heading out to the main channel. The Mississippi was flat as a mirror except for ripples near the shore caused by submerged rocks or dead tree branches. As the nose of the boat hit the main stream we could feel the force of the current causing Schlitz to grunt and dig deeper with the oars. The grunting, the squeak of the oar locks and the slight bubbling at the bow of the boat, were the only sounds. There was no breeze. My nostrils filled with the perfume of nocturnal river air, a mix of decaying leaves, mud and bull rushes. There was a faint hint of smoke from some distant, unseen fire. We felt immensely happy to be on the river in our quest for ducks.

We arrived at the mouth of the Cannon a little ahead of schedule. Most likely this was the result of the absence of wind combined with the work of the enthusiastic oarsman. On entering the Cannon we could feel the increased current. Immediately we headed for the right hand shore and grabbed a tree limb while I took over the oars.

There was no other light than the stars. The dense forest created a canopy making it so dark that Schlitz had to periodically shine his flashlight while I pulled mightily on the oars. My exertion was such that shortly I broke a sweat. In quick succession I removed my heavy hunting jacket; then off came my flannel shirt so that I finally labored in only my undershirt, quite unusual for duck hunting weather. A sudden slap of a beaver tail next to the boat startled us. It sounded like a shot gun discharging.

Due to the faster current and difficulty navigating the many bends in the inky black night, our time to reach Spring Creek Lake took longer than planned. However, the shorter than anticipated first leg compensated for it and we arrived at the entrance to Spring Creek Lake right on schedule. As we entered, the current abated. The water was now shallow so we could pole with our disengaged oars through the dense bull rushes.

A faint glow appeared in the east as we finally gained our planned site among the high, fragrant rushes. We cut a number of clusters to camouflage ourselves and the green boat. The glow expanded into an orange bloom as we settled back against cushions, Schlitz in the stern, I in the bow. Our loaded shot guns rested on our laps. We waited.

The stars slowly blurred and disappeared into an azure sky as a sharp rim of the sun sliced above the trees. All was still. It was to be a brilliant, clear, warm October day coveted by hikers, tennis players and golfers but not by duck hunters. No ducks could be seen. As our excitement dissipated in the reality of our situation our eyes became heavy with sleep. We tried to combat our somnolence with hot coffee poured from a thermos jug. Ice cold lemonade would have been more appropriate. The meat sandwiches prepared in abundance tasted dry and uninteresting. A few bites and our hunger fled. Our eye lids became heavier. There was nothing to do but wait. By eight o'clock the sun glared at us. We sat in our undershirts. Our gun barrels were hot but not from firing. Our early rising and nocturnal toil were now taking their toll. Even the slight breeze that rattled the rushes could not keep us from sleep.

It was such pleasant sleep. Periodically I partially awakened to smell the rushes and feel the caress of the sun. Then back to sleep. I shouldn't sleep. That's not the way to hunt ducks. I should stay alert. These thoughts were repeatedly overcome by the pleasant warmth and fragrance that enveloped us.

Suddenly, as though I had been dumped in the water, I woke up, completely alert. As I lay against the cushion, my legs stretched out flat on the floor of the boat, my line of sight projected directly over the pointed bow of the boat. Schlitz was snoring behind me. I did not move. At a distance, a single mallard followed an uncharacteristic irregular flight pattern back and forth as though it were in search of something. I wondered if it could be looking for a friend or perhaps a secure place to land. I did not have to move my head to follow it. Then, mysteriously the bird settled into a glide path that would take it directly over the bow of the boat. It looked like an airliner on approach to a landing.

Slowly I reached for my gun and raised it to my shoulder. The duck's path continued unchanged. It did not flinch. I drew a bead and fired. In a characteristic grotesque collapse of death its wings folded and it hurtled downward, landing with a plump on my belly. Schlitz, who had been awakened by the shot, watched the incredible event and yelled out, "holy balls!"

No more shots were fired that lazy warm October day because no more ducks appeared.

On the way back to the harbor we took turns rowing. We had stripped to the waist due to the heat. The current was now at our back so we needed only to steer, allowing the current to bear us home.

The Late Christmas Shopper

My father was an intelligent, self-educated man. His formal education ended at the 8th grade. His early matriculation in the "school of hard knocks" was the result of two hard facts: 1) an economically marginal family situation and 2) the availability of good paying jobs requiring little education. The time frame was World War I. With his older brother he went to work to enable their younger brother to finish high school. In those days a high school diploma probably equaled a college diploma of today. The sacrificial act of the older DeRemee brothers indicated their clear respect for the value of higher education. It seems unfortunate that these two intelligent men could not have enjoyed the benefits of a formal education but they made sure that their younger brother would. They would lift him on their shoulders.

During World War II my father was in his late thirties therefore missing the military draft. He nonetheless served the war effort building and maintaining railroad bridges essential to the transfer of war materials to our fighting men. He could climb to extreme heights without fear making him a natural for his job. During the war his work carried him far from home often for extended periods of time. This greatly curtailed father-son encounters but it was better than his being in Europe or on some distant Pacific island.

When he was home he would take me to the drug store on Sunday mornings after Sunday school for chocolate marshmallow sundaes covered with Spanish peanuts, the ones with the red skins. Afterward we would often go to some remote hollow in the woods to shoot our Winchester 22 rifle. In the evenings he read books, good ones, not trash. Mark Twain was one of his favorites. He read Huckleberry Finn and Tom Sawyer to me as I sat on his lap. I am certain my love of books came from these valuable sessions. I sensed my mother never quite accepted or understood her scholarly husband who may have neglected her for his books.

Following World War II he decided to leave the itinerant life of a railroad bridge builder for more stable work in town. His prolonged absences from home had created a strain I keenly sensed. First he worked as a carpenter's helper providing sufficient income for the family while he attended night school. My mother also worked as a cook and waitress at the St. James Hotel so we floated on the border of lower middle class. In a short time, father graduated with a certificate as a stationary engineer, one who works with boilers and power generators. Not unexpectedly, he was first in his class.

His first job was as chief operating engineer in a plant producing mineral insulation or rock wool. The pay seemed to be good but the work was dirty and hot and shift changes occurred every week. With increasing age his body and temperament became less tolerant of the rigors. Fortunately, he was able to end his working years in relative comfort maintaining the heat and power of the Goodhue County Court House. He retired at age 65 on his social security while my mother, nine years younger, continued working, now as a grocery store clerk. Sixteen months after retirement he experienced a massive heart attack and succumbed in three days. My mother was left with a modest house, debt free plus $8000 in savings. Fortunately she was able to continue working and to support herself.

My father was a laid-back thinker, you might say a dreamer. If he had had a college education he would have best fit the model of a college professor. In addition to having a fine mind he was an excellent athlete excelling in basketball, baseball, gymnastics and boxing. While I was growing up I heard many accounts of his athletic prowess that bordered on the legendary. In spite of his physical talents he seemed to avoid physical effort if it was not associated with sport. He seemed unperturbed by crisis. At least I never saw him animated during times of crisis.

You may question why I cite this background to tell a short story about my father. I think it is necessary to set the stage for this prototypical late Christmas shopper.

Being a family of Swedish immigrants the main Christmas celebration occurred on Christmas Eve. When I was a small child the family celebration took place at the home of my parental grandparents. When they became too old and decrepit the responsibility shifted to our home and to my mother. She would be busy for days preparing cookies, breads, and pastries. Christmas Eve dinner consisted of Swedish meat balls, ham, pickled herring and the *piece de resistance,* lutefisk. This was classic soul food for my father and uncles; they ate it in unbelievable quantities. All others looked on in amazement at their Christmas gluttony. At first I despised the gelatinous stinking fish but as I matured I grew to like it to the extent of still requiring it at each Christmas dinner. Maybe I do this in memory of my father and uncles but I think I really like it, at least once a year. With great clarity I remember my father eating 12 servings of his treasured delicacy. My uncles were not far behind. In traditional manner the fish was eaten with boiled potatoes and all was drowned in white cream gravy.

When all the celebrants were sated, the men adjourned to the living room while the women cleared the table and washed the dishes. No presents could be opened before the kitchen was secured. Exhausted, the women joined our cozy masculine lair. This division of labor is a throwback from Swedish farm traditions. I doubt it would stand in today's liberated environment.

After all presents were opened we went to midnight services at First Lutheran Church, the one my grandfather helped build but which he never attended. This Swedish immigrant congregation held some services in the Swedish language through the early 1940's. After church we returned home for late meatball sandwiches or rice pudding with lingon berry sauce.

I have strayed again from the main story in order to set the stage for the main actor, the late Christmas shopper, my father. My intent is to tell you about his strange Christmas shopping habits.

On the six days when Christmas Eve fell on shopping days, my father would start his shopping tour about noon. The merchants usually closed early, about four o'clock. About six o'clock dad came home with the inevitable sack of gifts. Mostly they were practical or curiously interesting and never expensive. They disappointed no one. The most treasured of my gifts through the years was a heavy, flashy metal belt buckle bearing the name "Red Wing" embossed in large letters. He expected my poor busy mother to wrap the gifts at the late hour which she did without noticeable complaint. When I became old enough I did the job with great relish.

It was not until high school that I thought to ask him why he did his shopping at the last minute. Given his relaxed approach to life I supposed his habit was simply a reflection of his temperament. He explained, with conviction; "First, things are picked over so there are fewer decisions to make. Second, prices are reduced if not drastically slashed. Third, last and most important, many of the merchants have a bottle of whiskey which they share with their old and late customers." It seemed to him an appropriate way to end a day of commerce and to contemplate the imminent warmth of Christmas Eve. All those reasons sounded good to me.

The Old Swede

Adolf, my paternal grandfather was my inspiration. He loved me dearly. Vividly I recall his funeral. He died shortly before his 90th birthday. His wife, Thilda, followed him three months later at age 87. I was 24 at the time. My Grandmother, Thilda, emigrated from Sweden at age 18. She would never return. Grandfather Adolf immigrated at age 2 through Ellis Island with his Swedish parents. He and Grandmother married on December 23, 1899 when they were 32 and 29 years old respectively. Thus, they were married just over 57 years. Their union produced three boys, my father being the second oldest.

Since my Grandfather was not a church person, his funeral was held at a funeral home. My Grandmother was a faithful and devoted Christian who regularly attended church until she became frail. Her funeral was conducted in First Lutheran Church where she was a member for most of her life in America. She was afforded the panoply of a traditional Swedish Lutheran send off to heaven. In contrast Grandfather's funeral was attenuated at best. I was proud and happy for Grandmother and the adulation she received. This saintly woman deserved it all. While I would miss her kindly presence, I recall shedding no tears.

My Grandfather's funeral was another matter for me. I burst into tears and sobs. My hero and buddy who built churches but never went in them, was buried with minimal recognition. I felt terrible that he was afforded such a perfunctory departure. It seemed unfair. Grandmother was a cinch to get into heaven; Grandfather's chances may have been less certain, at least in the opinion of many.

I never recall him declaring any religious views nor did I ever see him pray, even at meals and that was otherwise *de rigueur* in the family. His spiritual life was a mystery to me but I didn't think much about it because he was so kind and solicitous to me; his views about God were immaterial. If he needed a friendly witness before the bar of heaven I would gladly stand for him.

One of the flaws in his character that others pointed to was that he frequented a certain bar called The Barrel House after he finished work on Fridays. Usually he would come home late for dinner with what some referred to as a "snoot full." In retrospect this was what today I would call "pleasingly tight." If I were at the grand parental home on such occasions he would pick me up and twirl around with joy at my being. Grandmother would look on with apprehension as did my parents. I thought it was fun.

It was at The Barrel House where I entered the world of entertainment. Grandfather took me to that den of delight. He stood me on the bar with great pride and told his fellow revelers I would sing a song for them. In full voice I gave them my rendition of, "You are My Sunshine." The place burst into loud applause and for my gig the owner gave me a candy bar. Grandfather beamed at his five-year-old prodigy.

At other times we climbed Barn Bluff and looked out over the broad Mississippi Valley stretching beneath the brow of the hill. This river was like an artery issuing from his heart. From his youth through his old age it was on this river that he retreated for pleasure and solace. It was also the source of repeated anxieties for his wife, my father and uncles and occasionally for me.

Grandfather's youngest son, my uncle Everet, had a black cocker spaniel named Smoky. At the outbreak of World War II, Everet was drafted. His wife, my Aunt Gen, moved in with an aunt while my uncle was away. She could not take Smoky with her so Grandfather adopted him. Without question, it was one of the greatest things ever to happen to the old man. Smoky was always at his side and usually in his bed as well. When they were rowing on the Mississippi, Smoky stood soldierly at the bow wagging his stub tail. In effect, Smoky became my surrogate when I went away to school.

One particular river event persists in my memory. At the time grandfather must have been in his mid eighties. The Mississippi usually floods in early June from the run offs that occur in the spring from the melting snow. One June afternoon my father received a call from Grandmother saying Grandfather was on the river with Smoky gathering drift wood. He did this to build up his supply for winter when he used wood to supplement coal in the living-room stove; it was the sole source of heat for the entire small wood-frame house.

Grandmother was concerned because he usually returned by 3 PM. It was now 6 PM and supper was on the stove. It was about a 30 minute walk from the river to home. The Mississippi had flooded its banks and the current was fierce. It was no place for an 80 year old and his dog. She feared for the worse. Had his luck run out?

My father and I along with my uncle Herman, the oldest brother, went down to the river where Grandfather kept his old wood-plank row boat. There was Grandfather with Smoky unloading an unusually large amount of drift wood. He looked up with wonderment in his eyes. What was all the fuss?

He was three hours late because the strong current made rowing difficult. He and Smoky had to pull to shore occasionally to get his wind. He loaded the wood onto a wheel–barrow and started for home. I could only look on in amazement and admiration.

The old man and his dog would continue their exploits on the river for just a few more years. Then, after he was hit by a car crossing a street, Grandfather gave up. Although his injuries were not severe and healed quickly he was not the same afterward. Shortly Grandmother became senile and was moved to a care center.

Grandfather lived by himself with Smoky. My father and uncle visited him and brought food regularly. Then Smoky died and the old Swede sat in front of a window looking out over his back yard and the big butternut tree he planted many years ago when his house was new and his family was young. He smoked a pipe constantly as he had done since age 13. My father and uncles were concerned he would burn the house down with his pipe smoking but he didn't. Then he died and three months later my Grandmother succumbed not knowing where she was. The wonderful book was closed.

I'll bet Adolf and Thilda are reunited in heaven. Smoky may even be with them. Although Grandfather wore no religion on his sleeve he lived as though God had given him all he needed to be happy. He acted as though he were truly grateful for what he had.

PART TWO

From Mid-Life and Beyond

The Big Telephone Bill

After our children finished college, my wife and I decided to build a lakeside cottage, the one we had long wished for. Although we planned to use it mainly in the warm seasons, we had it constructed for potential year around use. As the winters in northern Iowa can be very cold we would either have to maintain upstairs heat to prevent the plumbing from freezing or drain the pipes to the basement and keep the temperature there at a marginally low level, just above freezing. Since the latter option was the most economical, it was selected.

Our cottage is located about 175 miles from home. It takes about three hours to reach by car. Thus, it is far enough away to give a sense of separation from our everyday activities yet accessible for long weekends. How to maintain some vigil on this precious property was always a concern. When I saw the electronic house monitor at a local shop, I knew I had found the security and peace of mind I was seeking.

The monitor sensed the ambient temperature and status of the electric power in the house. I placed the gadget in the basement as it would be the only part of the cottage heated during the winter. I could telephone my cottage to hear a monotone synthesized voice report, "Hello, the temperature is 60 degrees; the power is on, good by." If the electric power failed or the temperature fell below a critical level I could set, the monitor would call and alert me. Within a preset time I would have to return a call to the machine to acknowledge the report. If I did not do so promptly, the monitor would call again. If I continually ignored the calls, the machine was set to ring, in sequence, the telephone numbers of my three children and my brother-in-law.

During that winter, I periodically called the monitor, especially if a cold snap prevailed. I would hear the unpleasant but nonetheless reassuring computer voice tell me all was well.

One particularly cold early march night, things went wrong. At 12:58 AM I was aroused from sound sleep by the telephone. The monotone voice warned me, "Hello, the temperature is 38 degrees; the power is on, good by." Groggy, I fell back in bed only to be re-awakened within minutes by the same annoying voice. This time I was awake knowing I had to return the call to interrupt the sequence. I thought that was the end of it.

Just as I faded into sleep the telephone rang again warning me in the same steely voice that had now become a serious irritant. It had been only minutes since the last call. Dutifully, I responded. That night the telephone would ring at intervals ranging from two to 30 minutes. I was exasperated.

Deciding on a passive aggressive mode, I refused to answer. After the preset eight rings there was silence, but not for long. The next call came from my irate brother-in-law whose number was on the default list. I tried to explain. In the span of just over five hours, 32 telephone calls would occur as the result of the monitor.

The final call came at 6:38 AM as the eastern sky began to glow. I had been awake the entire night unable to do anything other than respond to the damnable machine. My feelings were a mixture of anger, frustration, self-recrimination, disgust, and finally amusement. I could actually begin to laugh over the way I was being controlled by the gadget. For what seemed only seconds, I crashed back on the bed only to be awaked by my wife. It was time to go to work.

What had gone wrong? A few weeks after that interesting night, I gathered myself to dispassionately evaluate the events.

I had set the basement thermostat too close to the alarm threshold of the monitor. When outside temperature was moderate there was an adequate temperature buffer to prevent actuation of the monitor. However, the night of the big telephone bill was unusually cold, driving the basement temperature down to the threshold of the monitor warning. When the heat was switched on, a brief warming occurred sufficient to shut down the thermostat. This was follow by rapid cooling. All night long, due to the intense cold outside that permeated the basement, the cycles were repeated, triggering the monitor. If only I had set the thermostat higher this story would never be told.

What lessons can be learned? The first is, be wary of gadgets you do not completely understand. What I should have known was transparent in reflection. There should have been a mechanism to disable the monitor and up regulate the thermostat. In addition, I should have made provision for some nearby person to check the cottage after an alarm. However, I doubt there are many who would want do it in the middle of the night. The most profound lesson was, don't allow yourself to be controlled by a machine.

Fortunately there were no more cold snaps after that long night. When I returned to the cottage I removed the monitor and threw it in the trash. It was not expensive. During subsequent winters I set my thermostat at a higher level and contracted a local plumber to make twice weekly inspections. I continue to learn.

The Ely Bath House

Ely is a small town, population 3968, in northern Minnesota near the Canadian border. It is famous as an embarkation point for the vast canoe country of the Boundary Waters Canoe Area or BWCA as it is commonly known. The BWCA is contiguous with its Canadian counterpart, the Quetico Provincial Park. Ely has the feel of a frontier town. Its main sophistication stems from the authenticity of the outdoor gear and clothing sported by the thousands of canoers that come each summer from near and far to enjoy this camper's paradise.

The town was established about the turn of the century as the result of the opening of iron mines in the immediate area. It has changed little since its founding. The wood frame houses are pictures of a bygone era. Some are dilapidated but most are maintained in the original style. Despite its aging appearance there is a vitality one senses visiting the small stores or mingling with the natives who conduct their lives with rugged self-sufficient simplicity.

In addition to the indigenous population there is a significant segment of immigrants from diverse origins and occupations. It is a common story to hear of the well-educated professional or business person who has abandoned a previously well-paying job to find refuge from the fast pace of modern life. Usually those immigrants were previously exposed to Ely because of a canoe trip or other activity in the out of doors. To the susceptible person, the attraction of the north woods can be overwhelming. It is difficult to identify the moneyed folk although there are many. They become easily assimilated into the simple, basic almost subsistence way of life that requires little cash to enjoy.

Whereas today most homes, even though ancient, have running water with appropriate bath and toilet facilities, this was not the case at the turn of the century. In order to provide at least periodic bathing for the dirty, sweaty miners, the Ely Bath House was established. There, for a reasonable fee, the grimy laborer could obtain a cleansing and relaxing steam bath and shower. Similar to the traditional houses, the Ely Bath House has maintained its original appearance and character.

The iron mine closed some time in the 1960's. This resulted in a radical change in the clientele of the bath house. Instead of grimy miners you will find the local business man, teacher, trapper, canoer or any kind of person who occasionally needs a shower. For the most part the customers are in quest of relaxation and interesting conversation.

I have been told the three main rooms have not changed in 90 years. The main steam room is low and dark except for the faint illumination of a single small glass block window across from the entrance and a couple of low wattage bare light bulbs on the ceiling. There are three-tiered sitting terraces along two walls. These terraces and the floor are covered with a mosaic of small square white tiles. One can easily see the numerous patches made over the 90 plus years since the floor was laid. The floor and benches are slippery when wet so caution must be observed on entering and finding a seat. Entering, you immediately notice a huge radiator hanging on the wall to the right. This is the machine that makes the enterprise work. It is superheated with steam. A spigot controlled by a lanyard on the opposite wall can be controlled by a bather to squirt water on the radiator creating a cloud of hot steam that billows across the room. Temperatures of 160 to 180 degrees Fahrenheit can be reached. Men sit stark naked around the room dripping sweat and periodically covering their faces as a searing cloud of steam envelops them. Each player has a large black plastic bucket filled with tepid water brought into the inner sanctum. This is used to wash the seat of the previous occupant or to clean a razor after shaving. A shave in such moist heat is incredibly smooth.

Customarily one takes three doses of steam for as long as tolerated. Interspersed are two rest periods introduced by a shower in the adjacent room and then by a prolonged sit in the dressing room. There one can drink a bottle of pop or beer and smoke a cigarette while cooling down. Here is where the conversation really gets good.

It is interesting to look around the room at the highly variable and often funny physiques … the fat, the lean, the aged and the wrinkled, the young and handsome. The patterns of tan or the weather beaten faces betray socioeconomic status but for the most part all are equal in their nakedness. Here you are likely to hear stories that are currently circulating in Ely. The story teller invariably laces his tale profusely with four letter words. Unless you are prepared or able to use four letter words your discourse seems out of place and you are quickly identified as an interloper.

How in the world did I get to know the Ely Bath House? My son, a science teacher in the public schools, knew he wanted to live in Ely. Like many of his compatriots he was introduced to the canoe country as a child in the course of our family trips there. He and his wife had to go through a few months of inspection and approval, probation as it were, before they were fully admitted to that unusual society. Now they are considered natives with all rights and privileges.

As a connoisseur of the local culture he knew I would appreciate the bath house and so he introduced me to it. Rarely do I miss an opportunity to go there on my visits. It is a bastion of old culture unlike any thing I have seen in the world. There is an endearing naturalness about the place. All the actors are stripped not only of their clothes but of any facade of education, social status or wealth. Here men are men. All is down to earth; figuratively and literally, everything hangs out. My son, the science teacher, says the bath house undoubtedly harbors some of the most pathogenic microbes known to science. Regular attendees probably own some of the most vigorous and broadly programmed immune systems in the world. He fears the business could be shut down if a public health inspector were to nose about. However, no one is aware of any health problems reported in over 90 years of operation. That's good enough for me.

One late February Friday night the snow was piled high and the temperature was far below zero when my son and I paid our $2.75, received two big bath towels and proceeded up the narrow, creaky wooden stairs to the dressing room. This is the anteroom I described earlier where you cooled off with a drink while listening to the local scuttlebutt. There are continuous wooden benches against three walls with another bench down the center of the room. Above all the benches are large wooden pegs for hanging clothes or towels.

This night we were in the first cooling cycle, drinking a can of beer while our sweat dripped to the floor. A rather sophisticated red-haired man came in, sat down to our left and began to undress. Recognizing some friends he immediately engaged them in conversation. In contrast to the usual diction his was grammatical but true to the venue, his sentences were laced and punctuated with four letter words confirming him as a member of the clan. "Well, we really got that woman with the —— pig," he blurted out as he pulled his legs out of his long johns. His naked friends listened intently as they smoked cigarettes and sucked on cans of beer. "Yeah, she tried to tell the city council this was one of those ——

pot belly pigs. She said they were considered pets, not farm animals so she had every right to keep it in her home. She claimed it was clear in the —— city ordinances."

I leaned forward and asked the authoritative gentleman how he got involved in such an unusual affair. He leaned back against the wall, completely naked, and said he was the —— mayor, not the mayor of Ely but of a nearby small town. It all made sense. He had the look and demeanor of someone in charge. He continued his narrative to a growing, fascinated and totally nude audience in various stages of cooling down. "Pot belly pigs are supposed to be small, anywhere from 20 to 30 pounds, about like a medium-sized —— dog. This critter weighs at least 200 pounds and poops all over, any where he wants. He's a —— public nuisance. Who in—did she think she was trying to fool, the —— city council? We told her to get the —— animal out of town by the end of the —— month or we'd send the —— law after her." As he spoke his face glowed with affronted pride and indignation. Then he paused, sighed and flashed a triumphant smile as he plunged into the steam. My son looked at me with tightly pursed, quivering lips on the verge of breaking out in hilarious laughter. He was able to restrain himself.

After cooling off, we dressed, returned our towels to the front desk and jumped refreshed out into the frigid night, snorting steam from our nostrils like two happy dragons.

Two Heroes of the Great War

Lucy and I walked hand in hand in the warm sunshine of a Minnesota summer afternoon. Our path led to the home of an old friend and colleague who was celebrating his 75th birthday. As we neared, Norm and his wife Char walked toward us with big smiles and outstretched arms to welcome us to the party. "It is great to be here, Norm, and hearty congratulations on your 75th." "Come in the house," Norm said as he beckoned us in.

Although we ourselves were in our mid sixties, I felt a surge of youth as I looked around. Most of the folks were in their late seventies or early eighties. This was a World War II crowd. Only a few were previous work associates of Norm's. Most were either neighbors or acquaintances from other associations. Perhaps their kids had been friends or they shared a common interest in the athletic teams of the University of Minnesota that took them on bus or airplane to important road games. Whatever the connections, it was apparent Norm had a broad circle of friends. These were all real friends with whom he wanted to mark his 75 years.

A bar was set up in the family room proffering a variety of drinks. To the right were soft drinks, wine and beer. On the left side of the bar, there were bottles of whiskey, gin and rum. Although a few took wine and beer or a cola, most elected scotch or bourbon with soda or water or simply on the rocks. Others chose martinis or gin and tonic. In other words, this was a real old fashioned cocktail party; the kind I thought was out of fashion. At least it was politically incorrect in a currently socially prudish culture. As a young man just entering my professional life, it was this kind of party to which my older colleagues introduced me.

The long cocktail hour followed by a sumptuous dinner with liberal wine became the model of our home entertaining for many years. The longer the cocktail hour the better was the conversation. It was conversation unplanned and unrehearsed that provided a convivial and interesting platform for getting to know each other and to meet new friends. What great fun these parties were. Never in the course of more than twenty years did we encounter inappropriate behavior or was anyone involved in a motor vehicle accident returning home.

Then rather abruptly it seemed this kind of party fell out of fashion. This falling out seemed to coincide with the retirement of the World War II crowd, the one whose company we enjoyed this late summer evening. There were other forces operative as well. The rising younger culture had other values and priorities. They were horrified by self-inflicted harm from tobacco, alcohol or fatty food. These lean and upright creatures substituted jogging or bicycle riding for the animal pleasures of the older generation. Of course they would accept the occasional glass of white wine or light beer or non-alcoholic beer at parties to appear sociable. Just one glass of wine for me, thank you. No, I have no need for an after dinner cordial.

I was caught at the transition. I loved those old fashioned parties. Now they were passé. Because I was still working at the transition point, my wife and I attempted to conform to the new paradigm. Only white wine and beer would be served. Emphasis would be on attenuated drinking and low fat nouveau cuisine all ending at a decent hour. No more morning headaches or desiccated mouths. Quite soon this modern version of the dinner party became a chore to attend let alone host. Thus, we evaded them, (at least I wanted to) until we finally dissolved into social outcasts, a status I did not entirely regret. It seemed that Norm's 75th birthday party represented a reunion of sorts of the old crowd who knew what a real dinner party should be.

After obtaining a large scotch and soda I moved about the room saying hello to old friends and meeting some new ones. Across the room I saw a beloved colleague and mentor whom I had not had not seen often since his retirement. With a smile he raised his glass and beckoned me to the seat beside him on the sofa. Not only was he a mentor but he was my hero as well. He had served as a navy medical officer in World War II. On D Day he was on one of the first ships, an American destroyer, to be sunk by German artillery. While ministering to the wounded, the ship broke in two, casting him into the cold English Channel. Two hours would pass before he and his mates were picked out of the sea. Even in the water he continued his ministrations as best he could. A number of the sailors died from hypothermia or wounds. For his efforts he was awarded the Bronze Star. Shortly after his rescue he was dispatched to the Pacific Theater where he was engaged in the fierce battle for Okinawa. My admiration for him was boundless.

While we sipped our whiskey he directed my attention to a tall stately man engaged in conversation by the bay window. He was gesticulating with his martini, almost spilling it upon making what seemed to be a very serious point. "He was a Thunderbolt pilot in Europe … never wants to talk about it … went through some horrible campaigns … lucky to be here." I turned to my friend, "you are also lucky to be here." He nodded with a serious look at the floor.

There must have been others at the party who had their war stories. Now they were safe in their old age enjoying a real dinner party that must have brought back treasured memories. The cocktails flowed for a long time as the din of the conversations rose. The food was full of fat that would frighten the less philosophical but it tasted marvelous!

I could not help wondering if the two heroes of the Great War had any current thoughts about the perils they once faced. When the shell fire crashed around them or when blood ran in the water or when a young man breathed his last, did they ever think or hope they would be standing around this room on a convivial late summer evening with aging wrinkled bodies drinking booze and eating good food? Did they wonder why they had been spared? Now more than fifty years after the great war that robbed so many of their youth these octogenarians did not seem to fear the long term effects of whiskey or cholesterol. At least, they hadn't been harmed thus far.

Battle on Kawnipi*

Along the Minnesota-Canadian border extends a vast wilderness forested with conifers, birch and aspen. It is set with a myriad of interconnected clear lakes providing ideal canoeing and camping. On the Minnesota side a large area is protected within the Boundary Waters Canoe Area or BWCA as it is commonly known. This is contiguous with its Canadian counterpart, the Quetico Provincial Park. For one who loves the out-of-doors, this is paradise. Here the body and spirit are refreshed in the quest for adventure in primitive solitude.

The physical exertions of canoeing cause what may best be described as a "dead man's sleep" when the day is done. What a joy it is to awaken from such sleep to the smell of freshly brewed coffee provided by an earlier riser. The aroma mingles with the scent of pine hung with morning dew. The air is crisp with encouragement to get underway but the taste of the coffee from a metal cup says stay awhile and be aware of all that is going on around you. Such mornings assure the voyageur of being in the right place at the right time. Can life be any better than this?

This is a story of courage and adventure that took place in that magical setting in August of 1957. My wife and I plus two other couples embarked on a journey with the destination of fabled Lake Kawnipi deep in the Quetico. Our starting point was Lake Saganaga in the BWCA. Normally the trip to Kawnipi should require two full days of hard paddling necessitating two camp nights.

We did not get under way until early afternoon. To enter the Quetico requires visits first to Canadian Customs and then to the Canadian Ranger Station in Cashe Bay. They are separated by a number of miles. Before we gained final permission to enter the park we would have to travel about 12 miles. Paddling at the speed of approximately four miles per hour it would be near evening before we could search out our camp site for the night.

The sky was hazy, attenuating the high August sun making it an ideal day for paddling. There was only a cool breeze, no ugly head wind to vex our efforts. The surface of Saganaga was like a mirror. We could drink its waters directly by simply dipping our metal cups. It was delicious.

The physical considerations of canoe paddling are significant even for young people such as us. Most difficult are the first two days. The muscles of day one are stiff and achy, requiring a number of hours of day two to unlimber. The "dead man's sleep" in between is a gift. By day three the body accommodates giving the canoer the confidence of an infinite ability to go on without further discomfort.

It was nearing six o'clock PM as we finished business with the Canadian ranger. Our stomachs called for food and our aching arms for respite. We needed to find a campsite quickly as they are scarce, particularly at the entrance of the Quetico. Most campers seek out their sites by four o'clock. Luck was on our side and by seven o'clock our tents were set, our sleeping bags ready and the other gear packed for the night. Our reconstituted dry food tasted as though it had just come from an Italian restaurant. It is amazing how the appetite rises during such exercise. As they say, don't ask a starving man to comment on the quality of the food so I am not really sure if the fare was in reality worthy of a civilized table.

By nine o'clock the mosquitoes droned toward us as the dishes were washed and stored. All went to their respective tents just beating the onslaught of the terrible bugs. There are only two mars on the face of the North Woods; they are black flies and mosquitoes. Fortunately, both pests are either active at certain times of day and can be avoided or they can be combated by chemical repellents. It is unrealistic to avoid any bites. The goal is to minimize them. Thus, with a low hum of mosquitoes outside the tent, the lonely call of a loon and a soft swish of breeze in the pine trees, sleep came quickly to us all.

The morning sun was bright and hot, quickly dissolving the dew on the scrub vegetation sprouting from the cracks of our rocky campsite. Quickly we struck the tents and packed gear as the breakfast crew made coffee and stirred up pancakes with bacon. Oh, if you could only smell the bacon over an open birch fire. It was to be a long day's paddle to Kawnipi; over thirty miles I calculated. Easily we would burn up all the pancakes and bacon before the sun was high. Our maps showed sixteen portages in our way.

At each portage the canoes are unloaded and carried on the shoulders by means of a yoke. The loose equipment and supplies are carried in canvas packs slung over the back with leather straps. Some hearty voyageurs can shoulder a canoe as well as a large pack. Being six, we had sufficient hands to make a portage in just one pass. Portages are often rough causing great strain on the feet as one attempts to step between logs, roots and stones. Shoulders burn with discomfort if the trek is too long. Mosquitoes attempt to rob you of your blood as your efforts to ward them off are compromised by the heavy pack or awkward canoe. Still, I love it. Hardship makes rewards even sweeter.

This was the second day, the day of pain and stiffness. A great deal of mental toughness is required to keep going at a steady pace. Our muscles argued with our psyches to slow up, take it easy but we drove onward stimulated by the prospect of great fishing in Kawnipi. There we would make a stable base camp where our muscles would have adequate time to recoup. As the day went on, our muscles began to loosen up. Our transit was going faster than planned.

At noon we rested after nine portages. Only seven to go I said to myself as I lay back on a smooth rock eating rye crisp, summer sausage and cheese, washing it down with lemonade made from the water in which we paddled. A cold beer would have been excellent. On finishing my lunch, I felt the warm sun mesmerizing me to sleep. The short nap was restorative.

With parchment maps spread out on a smooth rock promontory, we took stock of the remaining journey. Originally we had allowed two nights before reaching Kawnippi. Since we were considerably ahead of schedule a new possibility presented. By maintaining our current speed and skipping supper we could possibly reach Kawnipi by night fall. Everyone agreed we should try for it.

The final portage before entering Kawnipi skirts a water fall that cascades about twenty feet into a rocky gorge as the waters enter Kawnipi. Negotiating the portage requires a strong upper body to control the canoe on your shoulders. A sudden gust of wind or a misstep could easily topple one into the cataract below. We were up to the task.

The loons cried their mournful calls as we finally emerged onto the dark, cool waters of the long sought Kawnipi. This was a remarkable physical feat; it made us feel good. It was completely dark. Not even a faint glow could be seen where the sun had set some hours ago. There was no moon. Our only illumination was the dome of star-hung sky arching over us.

With flashlights piecing the night we sought somewhere to toss up a hurried campsite. It was after ten o'clock. A meager opening in the trees provided sufficient room for our tents. Hastily we prepared for the night, storing canoes and gear.

Hunger called out but sleep was more persuasive. Within minutes of creeping into our sleeping bags, the dead man sleep prevailed.

"Holy Moses, I can't believe this," Jim shouted. I bolted out of my sleeping bag. Only an instant before I was deep in sleep. Poking my head out of the tent flap I could see Jim on the shore reeling in a flopping fish on his bending pole. "What's up?" I called out. Everyone else was now peering out to see what all the shouting was about. "I've cast five times and I got three big walleyes." Was this a portent of things to come? Jim's third fish was flopping wildly on the flat rocky shore. He had tossed the other two in a patch of moss under a bush. Soon they would be sizzling in deep bacon fat for our voracious morning appetites. With a big smile, Jim exclaimed, "We've struck it rich!!!"

The walleye fillets were dredged in flour and corn meal then dropped into the fat just rendered from the large slab of uncut bacon. I assure you the crisp bacon was the hors d'oeuvre before the fish. Unless one has tasted this outstanding fish prepared by this simple method on the shores of some remote northern lake, you can't appreciate any hyperbole I might render so I will leave it at that.

Having sated ourselves, we quickly struck camp, packed the canoes and headed off down the narrow arm leading to the main part of the lake. The ease of the catch permeated my thoughts. Was this really a prelude or simply a fluke? It would not be long before the answer was given.

By noon we found a small island that would be our base camp for the next few days. It had all the characteristics we sought: appropriate places for our three tents, and an area for cooking and watching the fire in the evening while drinking the last cup of coffee anticipating sleep. The island also provided a huge smooth rocky prominence from which to slip into the cold clear waters of Kawnippi. Not least, the island gave some protection from snoopy, hungry bears that delighted in robbing campers of their food. Each night, as additional insurance, our food pack was hoisted high in a tree on a rope slung over a branch. Fortunately we were never visited by the hungry thieves. So, we were set for the fishing adventure we thought was ahead of us.

Jim's spectacular first morning of fishing was to prove the rule for the rest of the stay on Kawnipi. Each evening the wives readied the bacon fat and other elements for supper while we three boys indulged our angling passions. Fishing was so easy that only the walleyes meeting our increasingly critical standards for size were chosen for our north woods banquets. Even then, it probably took less than an hour to fetch dinner. All other catches were carefully released.

As is the case with so many over-indulged pleasures, a point of temporary satiation is reached leading to diversionary activity. The fishing was so predictably good that soon our excitement waned. Even the elegant taste of walleye began to fall dull on our palates. So, we decided on a little exploration into some of the interesting bays and tributaries of vast Kawnipi.

It was a snake-like stream that entered just to the north of our campsite that looked like a suitable object of our quest for diversion. After breakfast on a clear sunny, still morning, we packed a few provisions for a shore lunch as well as our fishing gear in case our angling libido should return. Our three canoes moved out slowly on the glassy lake, only the stern paddler working. There was no schedule to meet. The ladies stripped down to swimming halters making the scenery all the more beautiful as their skin drank in the salubrious sun. The men stripped to the waist. I needed only one long stroke of the paddle to propel us lazily a hundred feet or so. The only sounds came from a bubbling at the prow of the canoe or a swirl and drip from the paddle or the occasion screech of an eagle.

Our wives had not done much fishing but I don't think they cared much. Lucy decided to drag a line during our quiet journey. As her line played out I could detect an increased resistance to my paddling. Even though we had not set a schedule our intent was to explore, not fish so I became somewhat annoyed. "Lucy, why don't you pull the line in? It's slowing us up." "I thought we were in no hurry," she retorted with a bit of testiness. I dug deeper to overcome the resistance, not only from the fishing line but from my spouse as well.

About midway across a large bay we were traversing, Lucy's pole bent suddenly backward and our canoe stopped. I became more annoyed. "See, now we're on a snag." Usually snags in these deep northern lakes are large rocks. By moving backward or to either side usually suffices to disengage the hook. I pulled backward as Lucy's line passed forward suggesting we were directly over the snag. It would be easy to disengage, I thought. However, the snag did not release nor did it as I maneuvered to the left or right. When the pole bent sharply downward as the line whirred quickly from the reel, I came rapidly to the conclusion, this was no inanimate snag. This was a huge fish!

"Maybe I should take over, honey," I said with sheepish excitement. Now Lucy was annoyed. Reluctantly she handed me the pole, I'm sure she realized my muscle and experience would be necessary to conquer this creature. I mean seriously, this was huge. She might have been dragged into the water. Our canoe might have been upset which, given our position far from shore, could prove a significant problem if not danger.

Perhaps time has magnified the facts and the excitement my recollections evoke. It could be, but I don't think so. This was without question one of the fiercest struggles with a great fish that has probably ever been waged in the annals of fresh water fishing. None of what I relate is exaggeration.

Repeatedly I attempted to reel the fish in. Thirty feet of line would be gathered with great effort only to swiftly play out as the monster tested my weakening hands. I let him run for fear of losing the prize. For over an hour I battled on while Lucy attempted to balance the boat like a tight rope walker and the others looked on from their nearby circling canoes not knowing how to help. Sweat ran from my forehead. My hands and arms were reaching the point of exhaustion but I could not give up. I would not.

At last, the great fish also showed signs of fatigue. I sensed I was winning. Now I was able to reel in more line than before. He gave an occasional flurry of desultory resistance as I drew him closer. I could begin to make out a very large black image with a flashing lure in its mouth. Finally he rested against the canoe his black back just above the surface. Our canoe was 16 feet long. The fish was at least one third the length of the canoe. We all stared in disbelief. For a time I thought I could hear the creature breath. Its appearance was that of a northern pike or a muskellunge. Given its extraordinary size it was most likely a musky. For a fresh water fish, this was huge, I mean huge.

What were we to do next? You could sense he was gathering himself for another challenge. There were no means to land him in the canoe, no net or gaff hook. It would have been folly to attempt to land him with bare hands. He could have bitten off a few fingers. Likely the canoe would be capsized.

As the fish rested against the canoe I had the feeling he was studying us, preparing his escape. We could attempt pulling him to shore and dragging him up on the rocks. That was probably our best option if we were to escape our indecision and inaction.

I held the pole tightly as Lucy began to paddle for the nearest shore. With a violent snap of the head the line broke. The behemoth lingered a few seconds by the canoe. Then with a shuddering slap of its tail, he disappeared into the back watery depths. I leaned over peering intently for a final glimpse but he was gone.

A number of thoughts occurred as I looked wistfully into the water. They all seemed ridiculous in the aftermath of the gigantic struggle. If we had landed him what would we have done with him? He was too big to eat and besides, a fish of that size would probably have not tasted very good. It would have been unwise or improbable to portage him back. Perhaps stringing him up and taking our pictures would have given us some excitement; but all those considerations were moot. The monster had escaped. What happened was for the best. I thank the fish for providing such a thrill and a wonderful story to tell.

reprinted by permission from Boundary Waters Journal, Stuart Osthoff, publisher

An Autumnal Hawk

It was a classic mid-October day in Minnesota. The sun was warm. In the shade a chill prevailed calling for a sweater. Over the ground lay a profusion of brightly colored leaves. Hints of the transient nature of beauty were in abundance. Soon would come the calm seclusion of winter. This day must not be wasted. Thus, during my noon lunch break I left my office, drove my car to a fast food restaurant, got my lunch in a bag and drove to a nearby park to enjoy the fine autumn noon hour.

With all the windows and roof top open I sat back on my seat to eat my lunch. I was enthralled by the scene. As I munched my sandwich I noted a large hawk circling above me apparently searching for some small animal to sate his mid-day hunger. Serenely the bird floated on the air directing his flight with mere flicks of a wing tip or tail. He was directing a symphony. Strains of Grieg's Peer Gynt came to me.

Instead of coming lower he ascended effortlessly on updrafts. Perhaps there was no prey in sight. He twisted higher and higher, farther and farther finally becoming only a speck. Then he was gone.

I mused. The hawk must have been at work seeking to sate its hunger. However, he had ascended so high it seemed unlikely he could see small rodents or other morsels to eat. If he did, his extreme altitude reduced the likelihood of a successful pursuit. Perhaps I was naïve about the capabilities of hawks.

Such are the dangers of imparting to animals the same consciousness and desires of man. Of what use are such speculations? What do I know about the thoughts of a hawk?

Given the beauty of the day and the felicity of the hawk's flight I was convinced he was just having fun flying. He was not working. Like me, he too knew this day might not be replayed for a long time to come so he would take advantage of it. He probably had filled his stomach earlier in the day. Now he was taking time out to be aware of the lovely day just as I had done. I and the hawk were one.

Ice Chips

My wife's cousin and her husband were about 17 years our senior. I first met them shortly after our marriage. From our very first meeting we established rapport and mutual admiration. Bill was an accomplished man of *savoir-faire* and *savoir-vivre*. He was a highly intelligent and successful administrator, a raconteur of immense skill, a gourmet cook, and world traveler in addition to being a warm person and good listener (It seems necessary to describe him with many French words but I don't think he would mind that given his Francophilia).

At one of our last meetings and following a sumptuous dinner at one of his favorite restaurants, we looked at each other and spontaneously embraced with tear-filled eyes; such had evolved the warmth of our relationship over the previous 40 years.

Mary Louise or Bug, as she was affectionately called by her husband and friends, was a contrast. In many ways her personality was the exact opposite of Bill's as is the case with many long-surviving marriages. She might be described as uptight or prissy. However, underneath that protective facade lay a heart of immense compassion for public and private causes, and a disarming selfless toward her family and friends. Whatever the reason, I seemed to be special to her. Her opinion of me was extravagant and unwarranted but I confess I enjoyed basking in her praise. It was a tonic for my sometimes uncertain self-esteem.

Bug and Bill were in their 80's and because we had not seen them in a number of years we thought it wise to plan a visit. We lived in Minnesota and they lived in Washington DC; a significant physical barrier lay between us. The impulse proved prescient as shortly we were informed that Bug had cancer of the pancreas. Aside from some minor maladies attendant to an 83 year old body, Bill was in satisfactory condition to care for his ailing wife at home.

Our decision was galvanized by events. We had to go soon. A call to Bug, however, gave us pause. She was not up to company so we procrastinated. Then, on a late July afternoon, their daughter Barby called to tell us her father had suffered a massive stroke. He was in Georgetown University Hospital with a precarious prognosis. Meanwhile, Bug remained at home under hospice care. The next day we were on a plane for Washington.

Upon securing our hotel room, we rushed to the hospital to see Bill. It was a pathetic scene. He lay with a tube in his windpipe and a profusion of wires monitored his life functions. A prominent sag of his right face indicated the stroke. His eyes were closed. I spoke closely to his left ear and his eyes opened. He strained against the respirator to speak a few gasping words that made sense to us despite the lack of clarity. It was an indication he knew we had come a long way especially to see him. That realization was comforting. It was an absolution of our long absence. One of his old friends and colleagues was also at the bedside to share stories of this man who now lay helpless but who was still a vigorous presence in our minds. The visit was not long as Bill seemed weary and sleepy, as though the struggle was too immense and the reality too onerous for his consciousness.

Now we were on our way to the impressive home designed by their friend, the eminent architect, I.M. Pei. With measures of anxiety and dread we rang the door bell. Daughter Barby had been expecting us. She greeted us with a smile and hugs. There was a sense of stress and gloom as we entered the familiar foyer and proceeded into the living room where we had experienced so many memorable times. Bill's well-equipped bar was on the right. On the left stood his desk surrounded by his interesting library. I could see him working there.

Following our visit, Barby and her husband had plans to take us to dinner. As it had been the custom to have cocktails before dinner and despite the ambiguous circumstances, the custom was not to be changed. We were ushered upstairs into Bug's bedroom. She sat in a chair next to her bed, a pillow supporting her back. Three chairs had been placed in a tight semi-circle around her. She greeted us with a weak smile and outstretched arms. The bed was neatly made. She sat in a pale blue dressing gown over a plain white night shirt. Her attire draped neatly around her giving her the appearance of a classical Greek statue. Her hair was elegantly styled as though she had just come from the salon in preparation for an afternoon luncheon at some elegant restaurant. The scene was totally decorous.

Our drink orders were taken by the charitable hospice nurse who discretely disappeared to Bill's bar. In a short time she returned with our selections and retreated down the stair.

Having finished my scotch and soda I began to unconsciously chew on the residual ice chips, a habit not uncommon to me. That was about to change. For a time the conversation lapsed. A strained, disgusted look came to Bug's face. With flashing eyes she engaged me with the words, "Are you done chewing on that ice, Dick?" Quickly, with embarrassment,

I put my glass down. I experienced a chill, as though I had suddenly heard some bad news. Exposed and frayed by her illness, a long-standing intolerance spilled over. There was a silence. "I'm sorry." The conversation continued.

A week after our visit, Bill died. Two weeks later, Bug succumbed.

The Drawn Curtain

I must preface my remarks by the fact I was born into mild poverty. Although my lineal heritage stems from Swedish Nobility, dire circumstances dictated a modulation to relative insignificance at least as concerns matter of wealth and position. Into this scenario must be introduced the benevolent and rejuvenating influence of the New World, America. There can be no one who has more respect and admiration for this influence as I do. This stems from the fact that my ancestors forsook wealth and influence to seek adventure in the New World. They plunged into the equality imposed by their new anti-aristocratic society.

My paternal grandfather and his parents landed in New York in 1869. After the discomfort of processing, they headed west to the free and unencumbered shores of the Mississippi River separating Wisconsin from Minnesota. They bought a farm on the Wisconsin side just across from the milling town, Red Wing, on the Minnesota side. One can only speculate on the fund of energy and fortitude required for such an arduous journey to an unknown place far from a familiar home. Up to the present I have no good evidence as to what precipitated the immigration. In any event it happened and there on a primitive shore the family seeds germinated. I can not claim unfavorable events such as Indian raids and pestilence to have been operative in the character development of my forebears in America. The circumstances I have outlined them are sufficient. Whatever the influences that conspired, my grandfather became a man of great spirit, principle and vision.

Perhaps a consciousness of his aristocratic background instructed him. Among my earliest recollections of conversations with him was the subject of our nobility. He said I had blue blood in my veins and I should hold my head high. At first I was perplexed by the idea of blue blood since I knew it was red when it flowed from my cuts and abrasions. Gradually I understood.

Subtly, I was persuaded by my relatives (except my grandfather) to eschew our old world distinctions. This included discarding the Swedish language spoken not only by my grandfather and grandmother but as well by their children, my father and two uncles. I recall having no crisis of identity because of these conflicting currents of the past. I was clearly an American.

Where does all this rambling end? As I write these reflections I sit comfortably in the first class cabin of a jet about to land in New York. Behind me is a drawn curtain obscuring the passage from the coach passengers. How dare they look at what we are doing? My grandfather would have approved of my being in first class; after all I was nobility. I had just a twinge of guilt that I assuaged with my remembrances of coach class in my poorer years. So, what the hell, enjoy it as grandfather would have. This is America.

PART THREE
From Abroad

The Hotel Adlon

I first heard of the Hotel Adlon during World War II when I was ten. My father, who was an avid reader of current events, had purchased the recently published book, *Berlin Diary* by William L. Shirer. The book recounted Shire's experiences in Europe, and particularly in Germany, just prior to The United States' entry into World War II. His center of activity was Berlin where a popular residence for correspondents was the Hotel Adlon close by the Brandenburg Gate. This hostelry had also been a favorite destination of celebrities, royalty and nobility since the early part of the 20th century creating a mystique of luxury, elegance and mystery.

Although I was too young to fully grasp the significance of Shirer's reports I was, nonetheless, fascinated by the excerpts my father read to me. He tried to impart to my inexperienced mind a sense of the momentous events unfolding in Europe. The war at that time had not yet turned in favor of the allies. The possibility of war coming to the United States, and even to my hometown Red Wing, loomed as a distinct possibility to me. I was frightened. Living on the edge of fright and adventure created a keen curiosity leading me to page through the book when my father was not at home. The book served as a reference to consult as I listened to news reports on the radio of bombing raids on Berlin and other German cities. Such frequent handling of the book left it stained and dog-eared. It stands on my shelf more than fifty years later, its pages yellow and brittle, the original dust jacket near crumbling. It is a valued memento.

Why the name Adlon made such an impression on me I'm not sure. To pronounce it in German fashion, *ahd lohn*, conjures a grave, dramatic sound worthy of a Wagnerian opera. It had a serious ring consistent with the cataclysmic events transpiring in Europe. In addition, through Shirer's eyes I could see the frenzied activities of people under great stress, parading through the lobby of 19th century elegance on their individual paths to certain tragedy. Not least were my father's dramatic renditions and intense gaze as he read.

No doubt my father would have enjoyed sitting at the Adlon bar eavesdropping. He would have chosen the Adlon as his observation post had he been a war correspondent. Situated near the Wilhelm Strasse, the location of many important governmental buildings including Hitler's chancellery, the Adlon was the victim of collateral damage from allied bombing and was virtually destroyed.

When I arrived in Berlin in 1954 for my first visit, the city was in rubble. The western sector had begun to emerge but in the east (the Soviet sector) it was as though the bombers had just passed over. At the time, the Soviets had isolated Berlin in an attempt to stifle the liberal regime in the west sector. The city was saved by the amazing *Luftbrücke* instigated by the allies. Huge amounts of essential supplies succored the city on a round-the-clock basis through the Tempelhof Airport. The Soviets ultimately relented because of the tenacity of the effort and the negative world publicity the *Luftbrücke* created for them.

Although the Soviets had relaxed restrictions on travel to and from the city through East Germany, it was still cumbersome to travel there by train or motor vehicle. Air travel was the quickest and simplest way to go. Hence, with a $15 round trip fare secured from a student bureau in Hamburg, I and my friend Phil made it to Berlin. We entered through Tempelhof fully aware of all the drama that had preceded us there.

For almost two weeks we explored the shattered city. The Brandenburg Gate was almost black and extensively pock marked from shrapnel. The former Chancellery was nowhere to be seen. The Reichstag was an empty shell. Unter den Linden bore no trace of its previous importance and splendor. Strangely, that summer of 1954 I had no thoughts of the Adlon. If I had remembered to seek it out I would have found only a sad pile of rubble.

Twenty seven years would pass until my next visit to Berlin in October 1991. Shortly before, I obtained an illustrated map of the Potsdamer Platz area just before World War II. The map encompassed most of the famous buildings of the Nazi period. It also displayed a sketch of the Adlon. This time I went to the Pariser Platz where the Adlon once stood. There was no trace. The Wilhelm Strasse was now called Otto Grotewohl Strasse after the East German communist leader. The area of the former Chancellery was a desert of weeds and compressed rubble. The Berlin Wall had been dismantled one year before. East Berlin was reunited with the west. Cars poured up and down Unter den Linden from east to west and west to east. Only a few shops were open on the famous street, but the east showed clear signs of awakening from its morbid totalitarian night mare.

In 1994 I returned for my third visit. It was hard to believe it was forty years since the first one. East Berlin was on the rise. Construction cranes stood everywhere around Potsdamer Platz and Stadt Mitte. Never had I seen such intense construction activity anywhere in the world.

My fourth journey to Berlin occurred in September 1997. I had heard the Adlon was reconstructed faithful to its original architecture and elegance. I had to see it. My wife and I had one more evening before our return home so we would seek

out the Adlon. We were staying on the Kurfüsten Dam at the
Kempinski Bristol located near the west entrance of the Tier
Garten. The Adlon stands at the opposite end.

On a warm hazy fall afternoon we began a slow stroll through
the Tier Garten toward the Brandenburg Gate and the Adlon. The quiet beauty of the Tier Garten in the center of a
noisy metropolis encourages a leisurely pace with frequent
stops to inhale the wooded fragrance and observe the numerous crannies of fascinating vegetation. In just over an hour
we emerged upon the noisy traffic around the Brandenburg
Gate. The venerable Gate now emanated a warm ochre glow,
a sharp contrast to the depressing gray and black of 1954.
After cleaning and patching it looked as though it had just
been built. We emerged from the Gate onto Pariser Platz. Up
and to the right I saw a simple sign of linear neon displaying
the letters A-D-L-O-N. The ghost of Adlon was resurrected!
Crystal light blazed through large French windows of its facade. Inside I could make out visions of elegance restored. I
was in awe. I had finally reached my Adlon, a fantasy of my
youth.

Taking my wife by the hand as though I were a nobleman
helping a princess from her carriage, I beckoned her to go in.

The small lobby gave no sense of extravagance but rather a
quiet genuine feeling of refinement. Upon turning to the
right we encountered the dining room that minutes before
we admired through the French windows. Hunger mounted
as we read the posted menu and observed the early diners. I
approached the head waiter with a measure of anxiety since
I had made no reservations. "Is there a possibility for dinner?
I regret I have no reservation." I prepared myself for disappointment. His eyes darted up and down his reservation list
as he twitched his narrow mustache. "After eight thirty we
are fully booked. If you plan to stay only two hours, I can seat

you immediately." It was six thirty. "That will be excellent," I replied with undisguised enthusiasm.

A handsome waitress escorted us to our table against one wall affording an excellent view through the French windows onto Pariser Platz and the Brandenburg Gate. Minutes before, we had looked in through the same windows. Now we looked out with a great sense of having arrived after a long journey.

After taking our coats the waitress returned to ask if we would like a cocktail. Lucy and I both adore martinis, the American variety, especially before important dining as we were about to partake. "We would like two martinis—American style." "You mean gin with a little vermouth, of course. How would you like them, on the rocks or up?" (This lady knew her martinis) At home I prefer them on the rocks but somehow the ambience frowned on the crass American custom of ice. I looked at Lucy. She shrugged. "We'll have them up," I smiled.

Waiting for our drinks we perused the menu. As we did we also glanced around the peach-colored room illuminated with crystal light. We listened to the varied languages spoken by our fellow diners. Typical of good kitchens, the menu was not extensive. We finally decided on the recommended house dinner at a fixed price. I'm too embarrassed to disclose the amount of the final check. It was large but I paid it with no regrets.

The martinis were perfect, absolutely delicious. They tasted like more but fortunately the wine steward intervened. To compliment our choice of *pate foie gras Strassburg*, a mixed seafood plate followed by roast veal, he suggested a white burgundy. All wines were quite expensive. Hoping we would not drink much, we decided to order by the glass. The wine was most delectable. As it turned out we drank quite a lot due in part to the fact the steward made sure our glasses were never empty. His courtesy met with our complete approval. The wine flowed from the lips and over the tongue with the grace of an angel perfumed with flowers from Provence. It mingled perfectly with the extraordinary cuisine. What a fantastic dining experience!

We sat in utter contentment as we extracted the last drops of wine from our glasses. The dining room was now a sphere of peach candle light as we ate our mysterious tasty desert and lingered over coffee. It had passed too quickly although we had greatly overstayed our allotted two hours. The waiters didn't seem to care. I guess we seemed to fit in. Outside, through the French windows the illumined Brandenburg Gate shined in the night.

It was near ten when we finally pulled our besotted forms from out the Adlon's magnetic ambience. The long walk back to the Kurfürsten Dam seemed intemperate. Instead we strolled to the Unter den Linden subway station and took the crowded subway train back to the Bristol. Behind me lay visions of the Adlon, the great war that had come and gone; I could see my father reading Shirer to me so long ago; my youth had turned to maturity; I had an encounter with history.

The Imperial Bar

In the summer of 1975 Lucy and I went to Vienna with our friends Phil and Julie. The main purpose of our journey was to attend the Salzburg Music Festival. Vienna seemed to be an appealing starting point. Phil and I had spent time in Vienna as college boys in 1954. It was dear to our hearts.

After deplaning in Munich (also one of our favorite spots) we got in our rental car, a green Opel, and sped off down the Autobahn to Vienna. Phil and I took turns driving as the girls sat in the back doing things to keep us alert. Phil and I had not slept the entire night preferring to stand in the back of the Lufthansa DC-10 drinking beer, smoking cigarettes (you could do that in those days) as we did during our student days in Germany in 1954. How foolish one can be in youth. It was poor judgment to be driving on the fast Autobahn with our faculties impaired by fatigue. The alcohol, we thought, had dissipated long before we started. We became college boys again.

In retrospect it was lucky we had no accident. On a late, warm August afternoon our Opel came to rest in front of the fabled Imperial Hotel, our home for the next three nights. Our Opel was whisked away by the door attendant not to be seen for another four days. It was not missed. Traffic is dense. Public transport is excellent. I felt rather self-conscious approaching registration. Disheveled, unshaven, unkempt, perhaps even smelly, we were a bold contrast to the elegance of the Imperial.

A few words are in order about the Imperial. It is the repository of the bygone imperial age of Austria. It reeks of the *fin de siecle* decadence that created an incredibly creative culture and fine taste. The empire died but its legacy of fine taste endures. I continue to love it. Originally a palace inaugurated by Emperor Franz Joseph, it was transformed into one the world's most famous and comfortable hostelries. Adolf Hitler allegedly shoveled snow from the sidewalks of the Imperial thinking of the day he would one day cross the barrier standing in his way to the lobby. In 1938 he would stand on the outside balcony looking over the Kärntner Ring of the Vienna that rejected him, a struggling artist a few years before. The conquering hero-son of Austria was back in triumph.

We spent our first evening simply enjoying the accouterments of the beautiful, historic hotel, eating, taking a deep hot bath in the huge bathtub and falling hard asleep under the feather blankets. Much has been said and written about the hotel by musicians and opera stars whose venues, the Musikverein and the Staatsoper, are close by. Set Svanholm, a prominent Swedish Wagnerian tenor of the mid 20th century, thought the Imperial Hotel Bar was the best in the world. He had seen and undoubtedly sat in many. Nonetheless, with all the wonderful things said about Vienna and the Imperial, the real reason for telling this story is to relate a fascinating event that occurred one night in the Imperial Bar.

After a full first day strolling, visiting and tasting Vienna we returned in late afternoon to bathe, dress and prepare for a performance of the Merry Widow at Theater an der Wien. This theater, recently renovated, was the site of many famous premiers of Mozart and Beethoven. Following tasty, light fare at the hotel we hurriedly taxied to the Theater arriving just in the nick of time for the first curtain. This was Vienna and what better way to get the feel of the magic of its history than to hear the music of Franz Lehar. It was truly wonderful.

It was nearing 11 PM when our taxi let us off in front of our stately home. Of course we could not terminate this great evening so abruptly. A night cap in the Imperial Bar was in order.

The Bar is actually quite small taking up a front corner facing the Kärntner Ring thus providing a view through four tall French windows. All appointments were classic late 19th century featuring a dark brooding green as the predominant color theme. Valences and curtains hung like gowns of the Emperor. The bar itself is little more than a kiosk against the wall away from the French windows. It was manned by an officious dark-haired man of olive complexion, representative of the ethnic mix of the old Austo-Hungarian Empire. He was cordial but not effusive.

Our table, situated away from the windows, afforded us a view of the entire bar framed against the French windows. Outside, shafts of light darted back and forth from the passing autos. Our vantage point allowed us to inspect all the patrons' comings and goings. We were witness to a number of mysterious *tête-à-têtes*. Perhaps espionage was going on right under our eyes. There was a good deal of hanky panky without doubt. The place was seething with the out of the ordinary. The *coup de theatre* came next.

At first he stood wavering, touching the sides of the entrance to steady himself. He was tall, perhaps age 75. His eyes were watery; the lower lids sagged. Both cheeks were painted apple red as was his nose; the color was similar to that engendered by cold weather or perhaps by a predilection for alcoholic beverages. A coarse white mustache obscured his mouth. He must have come from a ball. He wore a frock, a top hat, a silk scarf and carried a cane like a field marshal's baton. Quite obviously he was drunk but he needed a drink.

The low murmurs became lower as all the patrons observed his magnificent entrance. A table in front of one of the French windows was free so he started his complicated stroll toward it. Disaster seemed imminent. He grabbed for any support along the way. Finally arriving, the top hat was placed on the spike of the coat stand after a few frustrated attempts. Next, the silk scarf was thrown up to the hat just barely managing to hang on. Jerkily turning his back to the French window to sit down, his body suddenly stiffened as it descended backward to sit on a chair that was not there. He penetrated outward through the glass of the French window on to the narrow porch fronting the hotel. A collective gasp arose as the old man catapulted out toward the street with a crystal crash.

The attentive bar tender decorously went to the scene and stepped out the patent window. Shortly he reappeared bracing the old man under the arm pits, straightening him to an upright position back into the confines of the bar and onto a chair. Quickly, two more men appeared in hotel service dress to brush away the shards of glass on the old man's shoulders. After replacing the top hat and scarf they took him out the door; to where I do not know but I suspect he was an old patron with a room.

Within minutes, all the glass was cleared. Save for the open window, all looked as before. All the players went back to their previous roles. All this happened within a quarter hour. Not a ripple appeared on the bar tender's face. Life in the bar went on as it had for decades. Old Vienna had come in drunk only to go crashing out the French windows. While most seemed amused, none really cared.

Belgrade

Every time Lucy sees a dimly-lit hall or room, particularly if the illumination comes from a single light bulb hanging from a cord, she says, "Belgrade." This reaction stems from a trip we made to Yugoslavia in the fall of 1990. Just a few weeks after we left Yugoslavia, the momentous civil war broke out, the reverberations of which are still shaking the western world. I had been invited to give lectures in Novi Sad and Belgrade by one of my old friends, chief of pulmonary medicine at Novi Sad. His sister was chief of pulmonary medicine in Belgrade so the rails were greased for a warm reception in both cities.

We arrived in Belgrade airport just after noon on a bleak overcast day, fitting for the bleakness of the facility. The building, equipment, tarmacs, everything oozed an overwhelming pathos. It was like going back forty years in time. Our previous experience in an Eastern European country had been in Hungary a few years before. Common elements came to consciousness; there was a dinge and unkempt appearance even to relatively new and modern buildings. It would have been easy to attribute everything to economic weakness but there was more to it. There was a palpable poverty of spirit, at least on the streets, that accentuated the economic short comings. It would not have surprised me to see similar scenes in any of the former East Block communist countries. Such were the contributions of communism to the world.

After an exciting trip by car to Novi Sad, our driver took us to Petrovaradin, an old fortress in the days of Austrian hegemony, now converted from a barracks and stable into a pleasant hotel with a feel of one hundred years ago. It was suggested we take a rest and prepare for dinner with our host at seven o'clock.

A gentle rain fell outside our cozy open window looking across the Sava River. The large bridge crossing the Sava would subsequently appear in newspapers and television having been destroyed by precision bombing. At that moment we knew nothing of what would shortly happen so we fell fast asleep, the rain chanting softly to our tired bodies.

I will not recount all the wonderful and satisfying entertainment and hospitality we received because I want to get back to the feeling of "Belgrade." The night before our departure, we were to be guests of Olga (the chief in Belgrade and sister of my host) in her apartment. Our plane from Dubrovnik— where we were on a brief pleasure tour– did not arrive until 8:15 PM. Thus, it was late, about 9:00 PM, when we arrived by car, again in a misty rain. The streets were mostly dark with only an occasional dim street light. The apartment building appeared to be of turn of the century vintage, an example of the architecture of the late Austrian Empire. It was too dark to appreciate any details. After pressing the button by her apartment listing, a coarse buzz unlatched the heavy wooden door admitting us to a dim gloom that took minutes to pierce. A sterile, unpainted wooden staircase beckoned us upward. Over the first landing a dim bare bulb, perhaps no more than 40 Watts, hung from a long frayed twisted cord. It was the sole illumination. It appeared that the entrance way and stairs were only rarely cleaned. A heavy musty smell caused Lucy to breath through her mouth. Upward we ascended, our shoes grinding on the grit.

On reaching the top we were enveloped in relative darkness. Even the dim bulb one flight below did little to help us see what lay before us. The well of a large door was just discernible. Feeling along the wall my hand dropped into the casing and I could feel what seemed to be a door knocker. Cautiously I moved it and heard the echo of a hammer against a bell. Presently the door swung wide with a cheerful Slavic welcome from Olga. Only her outline was visible to us as we squinted against a brighter light coming from her apartment. "Welcome. I hope you had a good time in Dubrovnik." "Thank you, Olga. We had a marvelous time. Dubrovnik is an exquisite city," I replied.

Waiting to greet us was her brother, our old friend and colleague who we left two days ago. "Greetings, Dick and Lucy. I had a call from Mira (his friend who took care of us in Dubrovnik). She said you all had a lovely, exciting time together." "It was just great, Brani. Thanks so much for connecting her to us." "Don't mention it. Who knows, she may come to see you some day." "We would be delighted to do anything to reciprocate her excellent hospitality."

In her deep Slavic accent, Olga bid us to her parlor. My first impression was we were in a mausoleum. The ceilings must have been four meters high. The walls were clad in dark green wall paper bearing embossments of flowers. Shiny mauve drapes and valences framed the two huge windows that started from the top of the ceiling and extended to a platform the proper height for sitting and peering out the window. Only specks of light and an occasional pair of auto headlights broke through the blackness outside the windows this night. I looked out briefly, turned back to the hostess and said, "What a lovely apartment you have." "Thank you, Dick. It is my pleasure to share it with you and Lucy this evening."

The room was absolutely fascinating. Again I was thrown back in time, not just 40 years but a hundred years. A veritable museum of relics from the past hung from walls, peered out of crannies, sat on aged tables; Swords, old armor, wood reliefs of heroic battles all scattered about as though they were just dumped; perhaps there was a plan to organizing them some day and assign each piece a specific location but not right now.

Slivovitz was proffered before dinner. I thought that was something for after dinner but I was not about to object. A hefty drink was in order after the long travel. The dankness of the night, the mystery of this place and the fascination of these people demanded a drink. With glasses raised we saluted each other. After taking a generous swallow, I choked. My eyes watered as I tried to suppress a cough. This brought laughter to the room. Brani rejoined, "Powerful stuff, Dick, for powerful people." "You are absolutely right, Brani," I said as I wiped tears from my eyes.

It must have been after 10 o'clock when we finished our drinks and were ushered in to the dining room. It was a tight room, just enough room to circulate behind the chairs but no more. Aside from the high ceiling and pea-green paint there were no memorable features. A few small oil paintings of no distinction broke up the walls.

A first course consisted of cold crab meat salad with cold vegetables. A hot meal would have pleased me more but the lack of food during the day left me with a hunger that transcended my culinary snobbery and I ate heartily. It was not like eating at Maxims but after all, we were in the Balkans where tastes may not be the same. Actually, I didn't know this was a first course or only course. Had I known this fact I would have left some space in my stomach. Next, came a whole leg of lamb, cold and ringed by a fiery column of red peppers. I struggled this time to look appreciative. Inside, I was churning. Anywhere but here I would rather have been. I choked it down. Next, for dessert came a huge torte covered with chestnut paste mounded with whipped cream. Lucy and I were both in agony as we tried to please our hostess while not allowing ourselves to become sick. We had simply eaten too much of the first course. I had visions of excusing myself to vomit.

It was nearing mid-night as we sat around the table sipping coffee and eating small chocolates when a sudden interruption occurred. Noise and agitation came from the entrance to the apartment. The great door slammed shut followed by the clump of heavy shoes. Presently, two young men hesitated briefly at the dining room entrance scanning the table. Olga looked up impassively saying nothing. The taller man with scraggly black hair and beard nodded and disappeared behind a door and was not seen again. Olga said something to the shorter fellow who gave a brief reply and nervously seated himself next to her, drawing a plate beneath his face. He was hungry. His eyes darted quickly around the room but engaged no one. He seemed oblivious of anyone in the room save Olga. A crew cut framed his head. He had not shaved for days. It was not a formal beard that he was attempting. I suspect he simply neglected to shave.

Olga served him food. She said nothing to us about him. She didn't try to introduce him. Lucy and I must have looked aghast at what was happening. We were lost for words or even appropriate gestures like stage-frightened teenagers. Strangely, with bowed arms he devoured the food in just a few minutes, wiped his chin on a sleeve, thrust his chair backward and with a grunt disappeared behind the door his colleague had used and was seen no more.

Our table conversation continued as though the strange intrusion had not happened. Lucy and I exchanged subtle (I hope) glances of disbelief.

The evening ended amicably around mid-night. The next afternoon, Olga took us for a tour of the city before taking us to the train station for our overnight sleeper train to Venice. We said fond farewells to Brani as he had to go back to work in Novi Sad. He would drive there that night. He had been a great host.

It was difficult to go to sleep that night because of the strange happening in Olga's apartment. In fact I still think of it from time to time. My guess is that the strange diner was Olga's son. The other person was his guardian, chaperone or simply a solicitous friend. Maybe they had been drinking and perhaps too much. What a strange night.

At nine PM we said goodbye to Olga as we boarded the sleeper train. Belgrade station is unusual. Passing through a masonry facade that looks like the entrance of a large public building, one steps onto an open air unpaved plaza set with rows of railroad tracks serving as embarking platforms. The area was dimly lit by a few widely dispersed large bulbs reflecting against crenulated circular reflectors. A considerable climb was necessary to gain entrance to our waiting Wagon Lits. A high whistle sounded and we lurched forward into the darkness.

Although our berths were prepared for sleep we stayed up to observe the passing scene. Dimly lit windows, dimly lit crossings, even a dimly lit train corridor entranced me. During the night I awakened when the train stopped at places such as Zagreb and Ljubljana. Morning broke in bright sunshine to welcome us to Trieste. With great excitement we anticipated our imminent arrival in Santa Lucia train station to see our old friend, Venice.

The World's Worst Toilet

I know this is a crazy subject but I find it interesting and not a bad way to remember events and places. As much as I like and seek out pleasant smells I spend as much effort trying to avoid the bad ones, especially those associated with human life functions, if you know what I mean. Most of my memorable bad odors were experienced during my travels in Europe that I started as a student in 1954. With no difficulty at all I recall one hot September in Venice when the city was steaming and its canals simmered like pots of soup. In the small neighborhood canals that bore only occasional traffic, the garbage and flotsam accumulated into small rafts of corruption. The September sun baked these rafts like crusts on a pie or parmesan cheese floating on French onion soup under a broiler. Under these circumstances fermentation and breakdown worked their ways to the fullest with an expected result—horrendous odors wafting over the otherwise picturesque views. Emerging from a dark and relatively cool cali I bounded up the small arching bridge crossing one of these small stagnant canals. The view caught me. I stopped to take it in. Just-washed clothes hung from lines stretched between windows. Wooden boats unloaded supplies to the local businesses maneuvering between rafts of debris. Then a breeze swept toward me carrying a mixture of scents and odors previously untested. In an instant I turned my head 180 degrees from this previously enchanting vista. I retched and nearly vomited as I fled down the bridge into the cali. This was just the beginning of a repertoire of smells I was to collect over the next forty plus years. It was the beginning of a genre of experience I associated with travel.

Lucy contends the worst smells she experienced were on a trip to a remote village in the Northern Territories of Hong Kong. There were two shacks, one for men the other for women just outside the bus stop so it was convenient. Inside there was no evidence of attempts to clean them. They were like conventional American outhouses with holes in a board seat. Waste was so high it almost protruded through the holes. I admit, her candidate for the worst in the world is a strong one (no pun intended) but I'll rest with mine.

As the story unfolds I believe the reader will understand my selection. The criteria developed post hoc because no one could ever imagine the nuances of toilet smells before they have been experienced. I suspect there are still some smells awaiting me that may put my champion to shame. I'll just have to wait and see (and smell).

Our hydrofoil from Vienna was slowing for a landing at a quay in Budapest on a warm and sunny September afternoon. All passengers were jostling to be the first to disembark but we were in no hurry so we lingered in our seats to watch the interesting skyline and observe docking procedures. Now it was our turn to cross the heaving gangway, virtually the last of the passengers. A taxi stand was nearby but the urge to re-lieve myself was too strong to endure the ride to the hotel so I made the decision to head where the sign pointed. I don't know why I hadn't used the facilities on the boat. I guess I was too involved with scenery and the activity of the crew. Lucy waited with the luggage.

If memory serves correctly, the destination of my wants was about 100 yards away. It was a stone block building sited on the very edge of the quay. I suspect that was deliberate to avoid the necessity of pipes to the main sewage system. The compelling feature of this Budapest WC was the force of the smell. Yes, I mean force, not just the strength of the smell but it had force like a wind blowing at you. About 50 yards out I had to bend forward against the force of the smell as though I was walking against a gale force wind. Do I really want to do this? I had to. Just open your mouth like Lucy does to short circuit the smell. I did that but it didn't help. That maneuver only caused a bad taste.

Onward I pressed. My eyes started to water. I was becoming nauseated but it was either going to be in there or right on the quay in broad daylight. My mid-western modesty prevailed to propel me through the door. What I saw inside I will not relate. It was too ghastly, too disgusting. You could have done it any where and I quickly did as a wave of nausea gripped me as it had that day in Venice. Wheeling about on a sliding heel I bolted out the door assisted by the force I previously described. No time was taken to zip up. That would have been a foolish pause. I may not have made it. Running back to Lucy I could see a concerned look on her face. "What in the world happened?" "It's too painful to tell you now. Let's get a cab."

Regrouping around a beer at our hotel I related the terrible tale. She was not impressed and quickly recalled the one in Hong Kong. No, this was of an entirely different magnitude of gore. I respected her story but she had not experienced this one first hand as I had. We both decided to drop it. Our beers didn't seem to taste as good after this talk.

Oh, how I empathize with Budapest that must endure the ignominy of having the worst toilet in the world. Somehow, some day the city fathers will have to come to grips with this natural disaster if any are brave enough to get near it. Oh, Budapest, I weep for you.

Paris, Afternoon and Evening

Paris in late June 1995 was hot. For many consecutive days the temperature hovered between 90 and 100 degrees Fahrenheit. I was met by a blast of hot air as I emerged from my plane at Charles De Gaul airport. A short bus ride took me to a commuter train that in turn brought me to the efficient Metro system.

As I emerged from the Luxembourg Metro station I could smell car exhaust commingled with Gauloises cigarette smoke. Herds of cars and motor bikes honked and whirred by on Boulevard St. Michel. Across the street stood Luxembourg Garden neatly trimmed. Paris embraced me.

This was my sixth trip to Paris since my college days in 1954. Since that first visit I harbored ambivalence toward the City and its citizens. The unmatched beauty and excitement of Paris had always been an attraction. However, I found the Parisians to be a testy, indifferent lot, wholly inimical to my midwestern canon of behavior. On each return I was guarded, preparing for more vexations. I had to accommodate my love for the physical beauty to my antipathy for its denizens. On this my sixth visit wariness dissipated into a mellow acceptance. I forced myself to try to understand the culture lest I be rejected by this astonishingly beautiful city.

Armed with my reborn tolerance I dragged my luggage down the busy boulevard past the numerous sidewalk cafes bustling with mid-day refugees from the hot sun. They sat smoking

Gauloises and drinking beer attempting to assuage the sun god from the wrath he was visiting on Paris. My destination was the Hotel Trianon St. Michel just five blocks from the metro station.

As I struggled on, I was surprised to be greeted by a group of colleagues holding out in one of the cafes. I had last seen them at a meeting at Cambridge University two years before. Now we were gathering in Paris to continue a series of scientific meetings that had taken place periodically for almost ten years. It would attract scientists from all over the world. They greeted me and invited me to join them. Desperately desiring to replace my voluminous sweat I looked longingly at their tall beers. I almost weakened. "Great to see you all. Sorry I can't join you but I've got an appointment in just under two hours. I must get cleaned up. Thanks. See you later." I had been invited to a welcome dinner party in a restaurant on the left bank and I did not want to be late. Not only was I thirsty but exceedingly hungry as well.

The Hotel Trianon St. Michel should not be confused with the one with a similar name elsewhere in the city. My Trianon had an inauspicious entrance covered by the ubiquitous shiny canvas canopy. Astonishingly, the concierge and desk clerk welcomed me with a smile and pleasant, *bon jour*. Was I dreaming? I am pleased to report the same congenial demeanor was the rule for my entire stay. I let my guard down and concentrated on the pleasantry that awaited me.

Within minutes I completed registration—again a surprise. The 19th century bird cage elevator was occupied so I climbed three flights of stairs with my bag to my room. If you can imagine opening an oven door behind which a combination of dirty socks, dried leaves and old books are baking, you will have a sense of what I encountered on opening my door. Not only was it extremely hot outside, it was more so in my room.

I was in trouble. There was no air-conditioning. What could I expect given the modest room rate for a Paris hotel?

After dropping my bag on the floor, I rushed down to the concierge. "Is there anything that can be done to cool my room," I asked in a pleading voice. "We will send up an electric fan, monsieur. I am sorry but that is all we can do. It has been so hot in Paris." I turned around in despair to return to my oven.

I was temporarily rescued under the cold ministrations of the shower. The bathroom was quite nice. It must have been recently renovated. Actually, the entire room was comfortably appointed, clean and well maintained. It gave me a feeling of the garret in the opera, La Boheme. But for the lack of air-conditioning, it would have been perfect. For three successive nights I would lie naked on just the bed sheet, the fan blowing directly on me and the window wide open. I doubt I slept more than two hours a night. By the time I left for home I was grossly sleep deprived but I didn't regret the experience.

Enter Ulrich. He came to pick me up and accompany me to the dinner at which he was also a guest. Ulrich had found an even cheaper hotel near the Jardin Des Plantes about ten minutes walk from The Trianon St. Michel. So off we went down the Boulevard St. Michel, Ulrich leading with giant strides and I almost running to keep up with him. I must have looked like I was jogging beside him. He was oblivious of my handicap during this or any previous or subsequent walks together. Actually I found it to be good exercise. The intense heat which had abated little, combined with the fast pace brought me panting and dehydrated to the door of the old left bank restaurant. It was air-conditioned!

Ulrich was 25 years my junior. Ten years before, he became a medical resident and spent time on my hospital service. Our affiliation turned out to be rewarding for us both. I like to think I was his mentor and he my protégé. On my retirement he assumed my highly specialized medical practice. The transition was seamless.

Ulrich was a tall muscular German who came to the States after his medical education. He had no airs or pretensions. He dealt with all people in a straightforward no nonsense manner. At times he seemed excessively blunt to the point of rudeness but it was just his way and I got used to it. A butch haircut topped his head and a shaggy mustache guarded his nose. What was most striking was his mind that understood all he encountered and synthesized data into creative concepts that he eloquently expounded to others. It didn't take me long to realize he would one day be a star. My pride comes from having played a role in his post-graduate education.

Much of Ulrich's secondary education was obtained in Brussels, Belgium where his father was posted as a German diplomat. French was the language of the school so I had a ready-made interpreter for Paris. Although he had traveled widely in Europe he had been to Paris only once and that was just a brief pass through on a school trip. Thus, as strange as it may seem, I, the man from the hinterland of Minnesota, was going to show Paris to the sophisticated European. I found it pleasantly amusing.

The scientific meeting concluded at noon Saturday. Because we were both leaving the next morning I would have about 12 hours to show my friend the joys of Paris. Before embarking we paused for lunch at a bistro near the Pantheon. The food was unexciting, saved only by the luscious bottle of white wine. Food can be inconsistent in France in contrast to Italy where, for over 40 years, I have never had a bad meal.

I had drawn up a rigorous plan. I pointed the way and off we went at a brisk pace. We headed toward the Seine for our first destination, Gare D'Orsay that had been transformed from a former train station to one of the major repositories of Impressionist painting. Even in our light clothing we soon became soaked with sweat in the blistering heat of the afternoon. This necessitated periodic stops at various brasseries along the way. French beer, in my opinion, does not stack up against the German variety but don't ask a dehydrated man for a profound critique of the beer he is proffered. It tasted marvelous, particularly drinking it at a sidewalk table that hot Parisian afternoon.

From the Gare D'Orsay, I planned a route that included Notre Dame, Montmartre, Sacre Coeur, Rue de la Paix, Arc de Triomphe and the Champs-Elysees. It was a superficial but representative tour. Most was on foot but occasionally we took the Metro. The heat continued. We were never far out of sight of a convenient brasserie.

At five o'clock as we enjoyed mussels on the Champs Elysees near the Arc de Triomphe a threatening bank of dark clouds approached from the northwest. The liberation of Paris—from the heat—was at hand. Shortly we were walking down the Champs Elysees as lightening darted and streaked through the clouds. As the lightening came closer booming thunder could be heard. Then the rain started, first in undulating sheets driven by wind and later turning into steady vertical showers as the wind subsided. We had no umbrella or rain gear so we ran from shelter to shelter, from awning to awning, doorway to doorway, tree to tree, anything we could find to flee from the rain. There was no hope of waiting in some café as this storm had the earmarks of what Minnesotans call an "all dayer."

By the time we reached the Place de la Concorde it was dark. Between frequent strobes of lightening and the garden of lights reflecting from the liquid streets, we walked and ran as though we were on the stage of some surrealistic play. I doubt there was a dry spot on my body. The previous heat of the day transformed into a shiver of cold. No longer did I crave a

beer. A hot toddy would have been preferable. My light clothing soaked with rain gave me a sense of nakedness.

On we went on our staccato path toward our hotels. About
eight o'clock as we ducked in and out of shelters heading for
Boulevard St. Germaine we heard beautiful piano music coming from an open door of a church across the street. I motioned to Ulrich and we splashed to the door. As we peered
in, rain dripping from our brows, there was a small group
of listeners sitting attentively near a grand piano played by
a young man. We edged our way around to the back of the
room as unobtrusively as possible; still we distracted the audience. Heads turned momentarily. The virtuoso continued
as in a trance. In the course of more than an hour we were
treated to passionate renditions of Chopin, Rachmaninoff
and Schuman embellished by the orchestra of lightening,
thunder and rain playing in the background outside. When
it was over we slipped out. There were no tickets and no do-
nations. I suspect it was a student recital. Once more we were
out in the rain.

Near ten o'clock we found shelter in a café at St. Germaine
and St. Michel. Before going to our hotels a cognac seemed
in order to leach the cold from our bones. Only a few customers remained. "Two large cognacs," I called out to the
waiter who approached our table. The rain continued pelt-
ing the awning over head. Between sips I smoked HB's as
we reflected on the interesting afternoon and evening. It all
seemed complete as though it were predestined. There had
been visions of beauty, smells and tastes, invigorating walking, a brilliant thunderstorm, and music all ending with cognac on St. Germaine.

I have the impression that Ulrich was impressed by my
guiding and knowledge of Paris. After the second cognac
and espresso we went our separate ways. The next morning
we met for breakfast in a small café near the Sorbonne. The

skies were clear. Already, at seven o'clock, the sun burned hot. The heat would continue. It was near 80 degrees as we sat under chestnut trees eating bread and marmalade and drinking café au lait. I looked around attempting, like a child, to memorize the experience. The next morning I awakened in my bed in Minnesota and wondered if it ever happened.

The Acropolis

I thought it a fitting conclusion to my 41 year career in medicine to go to Athens. It was there the mind of western man had been liberated as I was about to be liberated. Since I first became aware of the meaning of Greek culture to the world from my history studies in high school I fancied the day I could see this famous land. In particular the Acropolis with its crown jewel, the Parthenon, became one of the obligatory pilgrimages I was about to take.

It was just after 2 PM on Friday March 28, 1996 as my KLM Boeing 737 descended over the brilliant blue Mediterranean toward Athens. The ancient city was not visible to me because my seat was on the opposite side of the plane. I was greatly disappointed at not having an aerial view of the Acropolis. Even after landing and while taxiing to the terminal, the city skyline obstructed the view.

The old Athens Airport has the appearance of a third-world bus depot. It seems incongruous with the dignity of this cradle of western civilization. Customs was perfunctory enabling my rapid emergence into a bright Mediterranean sun. The sun of the Mediterranean is unlike anywhere in the world. It dazzles and excites. It stretches from far horizon to far horizon undiminished. To be sure, it emanates from the face of Apollo. Although the sunlight was appealing, the acrid air was not. It smelled of jet fuel blended with car exhaust spiced with human sweat. Fortunately the temperature was about 70 degrees Fahrenheit minimizing the impact of the smells.

I hailed a dilapidated taxi that looked as forlorn as the air terminal. "Olympic Hotel," I said to the driver. Off we lurched in a cloud of blue exhaust. The streets leading from the airport to the city center are walled by monotonous rows of business and apartment buildings of no striking architectural style. All seemed unkempt and dirty.

In my efforts to see the Acropolis I moved back and forth on the back seat but to no avail. The canyon of buildings yielded no view. We bounded and jerked onward in the increasing traffic. The driver appeared to understand very little English. My Greek was nil. I asked, "When will I see the Acropolis?" He motioned with his right arm extended, palm down as though he were patting a dog. I took that to mean I should be patient. My time would come.

Almost a half hour had transpired since we left the airport when the driver turned abruptly to the curb and stopped. He opened the right front window and pointed upward with a proud smile on his mustached face, "There she is!" In a narrow gap between buildings the gleaming white Acropolis jutted upward into the sky of Apollo. I choked with emotion. Finally the dusty pictures in history books were transformed into reality. I thanked him enthusiastically. He acknowledged with a condescending smile. He had been through this before.

We started out again finally arriving at the hotel near 4PM. After registering, I bolted to my room throwing my bags on the bed. I knew I didn't have much time. The room reminded me of the airport. The concierge informed me that the entrance to the Acropolis closed at 5PM. Fortunately the hotel was only about five minutes running time away so off I charged. I would have only an hour for my visit. My schedule for the ensuing days would allow no subsequent opportunity.

After buying my ticket I ran up the paths and stairs with a verve I did not expect from my 62 year old body. No chest pain, only shortness of breath that I judged to be appropriate. As I ascended the final giant stairs the awesome Parthenon flew into my sight like a monstrous ship plowing ahead on a craggy sea of limestone.

Only a few visitors remained as the sun approached the horizon attenuating Apollo's radiance. Now every shadow from the colonnaded buildings stretched over the precipice and tumbled into the city below.

After I walked around the Parthenon, I took a seat to the east of the edifice to observe the shadowy progressions. I was numb with awe. I felt as though I was swimming in a huge caldron of the past. I was given a new perspective of time. When Christ was born the Parthenon had already stood for more than 400 years. It was almost 2000 years old when Columbus discovered the New World. I tried to assimilate the swaths of history that occurred to me as I looked around the fantastic Acropolis.

Where I stood, great persons had walked and conversed. I thought of Pericles, Aristotle and Plato. I thought of the profound contributions made by Greece long ago. Our lives are so short and the struggle for civilization is long. As I left the sacred hill in the gentle late afternoon my thoughts were completely focused on the monument of time I was leaving. I wondered how far we had really advanced.

The Führerbau, Munich 1994

In June 1994 I returned to my beloved Munich in the company of a group of medical colleagues. We had come to attend a conference at which one of our older friends was to be honored for his contributions to medical science. On a free afternoon I led the contingent on a tour of places important during the Nazi times. Only a few of my friends had previously visited Munich and none had ever seen the places I was about to show them.

We started at Marienplatz. Heading east our first stop was at Tal Strasse 54, the site of Sternecker Bräu Keller where Adolf Hitler and his nefarious cronies established the Nazi Party on February 24, 1920. No trace of the original building remains. A McDonald's hamburger restaurant is now in the approximate location, ironic testimony to the ultimate triumph of systems.

Our next stop was the famous Hof Bräu Haus where the first mass meeting of the Nazi Party took place. We would go back on three successive nights to take in the ambience, beer and Bavarian folk music. Swastikas still decorate the ceiling of the huge ground floor hall.

Odeonsplatz and the Feldherrnhalle lay a few blocks away. It was here the beer hall putsch of 1923 ended with the arrest and incarceration of Adolf Hitler. In Landsberg prison he would write <u>Mein Kampf</u>. After his release his political career accelerated. In 1933 he would be elected chancellor of the

German Reich, the Third Reich. The Feldherrnhalle, originally raised as a monument to honor heroes of the Franco-Prussian War, became a favorite ceremonial site for the Nazis. Every year on the date of the event, the beer hall putsch was commemorated. The Feldherrnhalle and the Frauen Kirche are the two most recognizable landmarks in Munich.

From Odeonsplatz we turned left onto Brienerstrasse, a veritable doorway to a museum of the Nazi past. At number 8 once stood the Carlton Tea Room a favorite Hitler locale. I wondered what awesome conversations went on there. Just across the street is a monument to the victims of Nazi tyranny a short distance from the site of a synagogue razed by the Nazis.

A few steps farther down Brienerstrasse is the former headquarters of the Munich Gestapo. The building is intact and was renovated into an unpretentious office building. The wife of one of our group was a journalism student intent on recording our experiences. Valiantly she stood by the entrance to interview whoever might cooperate with her. She was able to question a few people about their knowledge of the building. The rest of us sat across the street admiring her determination. On returning she said only one person knew the building was once owned by the Nazis but that was all he could tell her.

Our journey finally ended near the Königsplatz where many political events took place on its vast grounds. The object here was to see the Führerbau across from Königsplatz on Arcis Strasse. Here stand two identical gray stone buildings separated by an open courtyard. As you face them from Arcis Strasse it is the one on the left, the Führerbau, that is of particular interest. It was here the infamous Munich Accord betraying Czechoslovakia was signed. Gathered here on September 30, 1938 were Hitler, Mussolini, the French Premier,

Edouard Daladier, and the British Prime Minister, Neville Chamberlain. It was in a corner room on the third floor that the proceedings took place. Old photographs of the meeting disclose a fireplace over which hangs a portrait of Bismarck.

Although I had passed by the Führerbau on a number of occasions I had never entered it. This time encouraged by the company I led and galvanized by the example of my journalist friend, we mounted the steps and went in. The building was now a music school, a so-called *Musik Hochschule* equivalent to the university level. Many students hurried through the halls so that our intrusion was masked by all the activity. Up the grand staircase we went to the room on the third floor.

Cautiously I cracked the door. A class was in session. Students were arrayed in a semicircle before the professors whose back was toward the entrance. Lights were concentrated on the front of the room on students and professor rendering the back reaches indistinct. It was difficult to see all the features of the room except the outline of the fireplace became clearer as my eyes accommodated. There was no portrait above the mantle, just cracked plaster. The door made a creak as I opened it wider causing the professor to turn a puzzled glance at me. Apologizing for the interruption I briefly described my mission asking permission to take a few photographs and then to leave. We would not stay long.

Graciously he nodded his assent as the student eyes followed us to the side of the fireplace. Their glances questioned our mission. I doubt they really knew the significance of the room and what had gone on there 56 years earlier.

I attempted to reconstruct one of the most momentous events of the 20th century. I strained to hear the voices of the protagonists, Hitler, Mussolini, Daladier and Chamberlain. Certainly the walls would still have residual vibrations of their discussions. Quickly I snapped a few shots. Thanking the professor and his students for their patience I led my group out onto the spacious stair case.

The reactions of the professor and his class suggested they knew nothing of the significance of the building and in particular the room with the fireplace where they now studied music. There were no plaques on the walls to recount the historical significance of the place. It was as though there had never been a Munich conference.

As they sipped their mid-day coffees in the canteen the students must have talked about the strange intruders. Maybe some asked questions of professors or administrators as to what we might have been looking for. Then again I sensed they didn't want to know. It seemed the Munich citizens who daily walked by the various historical sites we had just visited didn't want all those memories to interfere with the *Gemütlichkeit* they now enjoyed.

A Café Near Gar Ste. Lazare

It was like a gathering of birds before migration. The gathering point was a café near Gare Ste. Lazare in Paris. The time was late September 1954. Twenty or so of our group had dispersed from our disembarkation point, Rotterdam, four months earlier to all corners of Europe as well as some to India. Now we were reassembling for a last party before returning to our homes. All of us were college students from Minnesota. Each had designed a project to study in the field of the various European Countries of our selection. My buddy and traveling companion, Phil, and I had opted for medical topics in Germany. For two months we gathered information from many German physicians and health care professionals that would ultimately form the basis of papers we would write after returning to our campuses.

Shortly we would re-embark the boat, "Groote Beer" that brought us here; this time we would meet her at La Havre. It was from Gare Ste. Lazare we would take the train to La Havre, hence, the chosen site for the reunion of our fellow adventurers.

Phil and I came to Paris ten days earlier capping an extraordinary adventure sweeping through Austria, Italy and Switzerland. Near the Sorbonne we found a cheap hotel costing about one dollar per day. Finding such hotels near student centers in many cities had become second nature to us. Of course toilet facilities were usually down the hall as they were in Hotel of the Seven Continents. It was such an imposing name for such bare facilities. Nonetheless it was home and sanctuary. The floors were bare wood. There were two iron beds no doubt left over from the French Revolution. They bore thin mattresses stuffed with what we did not want to know. Young men always sleep well so no problem. A white China basin on an antique unpainted wooden table served as our hand and face washing facility. That was it. I recall no wall decorations, not even some tasteless picture or poster often found in such seedy places. But what the heck, we were used to such accommodations and this was the end of a magnificent experience. Soon we would be back in the comforts of our old rooms.

Nearby was the Café des Beaux-Arts patronized mainly by students from the Sorbonne. Accordingly it was inexpensive and tremendously atmospheric. For the equivalent of a half-dollar one could enjoy a tasty, nourishing meal including a small carafe of wine. My favorite was grilled pork steak with cauliflower drenched in cheese sauce browned on top. What more could we want? Just think of it, living in a left bank garret, eating in exciting cafes, sharing strange stories with strange people, drinking wine and smoking pungent cigarettes; we were living high.

Every day we explored Paris mainly on foot with the help of the fabulous Paris Metro. We saw everything a tourist should see. We did the Louvre, we climbed the Eiffel Tour, prowled Pigalle at night (it was safe then); you name it we saw it. Almost every evening we arrived exhausted in the Café des Beaux-Arts ravishingly hungry and thirsty looking forward to the denouement. As we relished the food, drink and environment ambivalent thoughts crossed our consciousness. Soon this life would be over. It would be cast into the hall of memory maybe never to happen again. Then there were the faces of loved ones calling us back from this fantasy. We had missed them dearly. We must go home. Yet it was no small matter to withdraw from the most exciting and adventurous four months we had ever lived. Our lives were changed forever.

Back to the Café near Gare Ste. Lazare. I do not recall how it was arranged for all of us to meet here. Maybe someone was tagged as the Paris contact. It is too far in the past to recall. I do know we sat on a warm sunny afternoon basking under a hazy autumn sky sharing our adventures and stories. In just two days the Groote Beer would pick us up at La Havre.

In 1954 there were three classes of train travel in France, 1st, 2nd and 3rd the latter being the least expensive. A so-called "boat train" was to leave Gare Ste. Lazare the morning of our embarkation arriving directly on the quay for convenient access to the boat. The problem was that this was exclusively a 1st class train. We could not afford it. I was nearing penury and Phil was not far behind. What little he had left he shared so we could eke out our last few days and hours in Paris.

In an effort to alleviate the precarious state of finances I had the brilliant idea to gather what funds I had and send a telegram home pleading for emergency aid. From the American Express office I sent a telegram to my parents with the terse message, "No mon, no fun, your son." The words were few to reduce costs. The next day I hurried back to Amex, thrilled to see the telegram from my father. It read, "Too bad, so sad, your dad." My disappointment was somewhat assuaged by an attached $15. It must have cost him that much to make the transaction. In Paris in 1954 for a poor Bohemian student that wasn't too bad. Naturally I had hoped for more so we could take the boat train but I was not ungrateful. It would help make the voyage home just a little bit more pleasant.

After retrieving the telegram I repaired to the café near Gare Ste. Lazare to join the party. As I approached, Phil saw me and rose to say, "Hey, Dick. Did you have success?" "Yes and no" I said as I told my story to the gang. Most of them laughed outright while others covered their snickering grins. They seemed to admire my father's terse reply and above all his wisdom at not lavishing me with large amounts of money. He knew I had my ticket home.

Despite the largess it still was not enough to cover the cost of the 1st class train and make allowance for certain necessities on the boat. Thus, the decision was made for us. We would take a 3rd class train to Le Havre the night before.

We arrived in the dingy seaport around mid-night. Evidence of damage wrought during World War II could still to be seen. In contrast to the salubrious late September air of Paris this was Normandy, an entirely different place, full of cold raw wind and drizzle. We turned up the collars of our trench coats against the inclement weather.

Fortunately, the Gare Maritime was just a few blocks walking distance from the train station. As we walked we encountered a drunken street brawl that we quickly circumvented not wanting to become involved. What were we to do during the long dark hours that confronted us before our boat would arrive? Where could we find a few winks of sleep? The cold stirred our appetites so we sought out the small bistro that glowed ahead in the darkness on the waterfront. A sign on the door indicated it was open 24 hours so this was just what we needed. On entering our nostrils filled with the aroma of espresso and cigarette smoke. A few round tables stood before the bar. On the opposite wall there were three booths to which the bar tender directed us. He had black curly hair with a droopy mustache tugging downward on his sharp pointed nose. His ancestors must have come from Algeria if he did not come from there himself. He spoke no English and we spoke no French. Using hand signs and pointing we eventually got ham sandwiches and red wine. Assessing our finances we judged we could still afford two espressos after the sandwiches. The strategy was to nurse everything so we would not have to go out into the cold night.

After an hour or so nibbling our sandwiches and sipping the wine we sensed the bartender becoming impatient. This was not the typical local in which to linger and especially at this time of night. Perhaps he feared some kind of treachery or had an aversion to Americans. He repeatedly mopped the bar as his eyes darted back and forth from us to his bar. On seeing us consume the last bites he hurried to our booth and collected the dishes and made gestures to ask if we wished anything more. I raised two fingers and said, "Espresso." We bought more time. Given the bartender's suspicious demeanor prolonging our stay was not going to be easy. This was not to be our all night refuge.

All told our dallying must have consumed over two hours bringing us to about 3 AM. When he returned it was obvious some kind of decision would have to be made. He presented the check with a thump on the table. After scratching together our last few Franks we attempted to explain that we were students awaiting our ship that was to arrive in just a few hours. We just needed some place to keep warm. He didn't understand or didn't want to. He grabbed the money and pointed to the door with a derisive, "Americaine" twisting from his lips. It was no use to argue so out we went into the forbidding night. We returned to the locked doors of the Gare Maritime and decided this was the place we should endure the night. Luckily our trench coats gave us a measure of warmth as we lay on the stone quay, struggling to find some sleep.

The bellow of a ship's horn startled us to consciousness. There she was, the Groote Beer gleaming in the morning sun as tugs pushed her to the dock. It was as though a great force had come to rescue us from our dark night. Our friends who had taken the high-priced boat train greeted us as we stood before them disheveled and shivering. They seemed relieved to see we had survived. In a few hours our boat steamed out to the big Atlantic homeward bound. In a little over a week we would be home.

I continue, now many years later, to think nostalgically about that warm autumn afternoon in a café near Gare Ste. Lazare. It was the pivot of our adventure, a point of gathering and going forth. What an unimaginable transformation had occurred in our young lives. We were not the same boys who left Minnesota four months before. We were better for all the adventure, all the self reliance, all the exposure to a different culture, all the exposure to beauty and all the fantastic food and drink we had experienced. The gathering in a café near Gare Ste. Lazare seemed to summarize all that had gone on before for all of us. It was a gathering of young people who had matured. There was the humor and irony of my father. Pervading all the conviviality of that afternoon was a subtle home sickness whose remedy was close at hand. Sitting in the café we were acutely aware of where we were and what great things we had done. The feeling was immense.

ADDENDUM OF PHIL ECKMAN:

I am completely enchanted by "A Café near Gare Ste. Lazare"! Your colorful narrative brings back pungent memories. I dug out my old travel log and was devastated to find that my journal ends abruptly on August 3 in Heidelberg; <u>nothing</u> after that! Did I succumb to laziness or just fall into a rhythm of the experience that left no energy for written documentation? How sad—but thanks to your sharp memory for the exquisite details (and perhaps more religious attention to a journal), these wonderful experiences come back to us. I am grateful.

Your description of the Hotel of the Seven Continents brought me right back there—even nearly olfactory. And the Café des Beaux-Arts—yes, I'm back there! I become vague on the details of the Boat Train caper—the lack of money and the telegram from Arty are clear. And the bistro in La Havre is fuzzy—I may have been "beschwipst". Crystal clear, however, is the sight and feeling of the Groote Beer coming into the harbor in the early morning light! A remarkable change from my notes of June 21 after disembarking in Rotterdam, viz. "We finally got rid of the old Groote Beer". Yes that journey was immense for us. Thanks for re-living it—and do keep it up. Phil

PART FOUR

Articles Of Faith

To Rise Again

The Apostle Paul writes in I Corinthians 15:14, "If Christ has not been raised, then our preaching is in vain and your faith is in vain." It would seem that by this statement, the entire validity of the Christian Faith hinges on the validity of the bodily resurrection of Christ. In this post modern era when there is a general disdain for supernatural ideation, the Christian Church is under attack from many quarters questioning its relevance in contemporary society. Given the progress of science in defining material reality, understanding issues such as the resurrection of Christ, the virgin birth and other miraculous stories causes strains that frequently undermine religious faith. Movements advocating radical change in Christianity seem to be gaining momentum. It is asserted that reciting a creed is alien to modern thinking people. How can a rational person assent to such ideas as the resurrection and the virgin birth? In the light of Paul's assertion it would follow that if Christ's resurrection is fictitious then Christianity is a fiction. There can be no reformation of Christianity unless Paul is not considered an authority. The would-be reformers are in a real sense advocating the creation of a whole new religion based on a non-scriptural re-interpretation of the life of Christ. By doing so they are turning a religion into a personality cult. They are shifting Christ to a niche perhaps no more meaningful than the veneration of other prominent persons such as Abraham Lincoln or George Washington. Certainly such veneration can give inspiration and guidance for daily living to many but can the reduction of Christ to a mere mortal worthy of respect serve the spiritual needs of people seeking underpinning of their lives?

Much of the controversy arises out of different conceptions of the function and importance of religion in human life and how the human psyche is equipped to deal with non-materialistic thinking. That many "thinking" people daily confess their religious convictions cannot be disputed. They recite creeds without the slightest sense of hypocrisy. Some might argue they are not really thinking but simply engaged in some sort of mystical delusionary exercise to assuage feelings of personal inadequacy. They may be right but they may be missing the point. Their reductionist view detracts from the mystery so essential to religious sentiment. How can we have hope of something better if we are entirely under the control of relentless physical realities? Where can we seek and find solace for the cruelties visited upon us by life if there is no ultimate author of consolation?

No matter how much scientific materialism may claim to explain reality there is still a constitutional psychic compartment that exists and requires symbols and myths for sustenance. For purposes of discussion let us refer to this compartment as spiritual/aesthetic. This compartment may be informed by the materialistic compartment but cannot be excluded by it. Let me explain. A case in point is that of the Galileo affair wherein he posed a threat to the church by his contention that the world was not the center of the universe. The materialist compartment informed the spiritual/aesthetic compartment and changed the church's view but did not destroy the religion. Some might argue that is exactly what should be done; to reform and not destroy. As will be seen later, I will contend that myths are essential to be maintained although they may be explained. It should also be said that the spiritual/aesthetic compartment can, as well, influence the materialistic compartment so that there are continuous currents between the two. I contend the two compartments co-exist and are not mutually exclusive. Pure scientists would have us believe that ultimately the spiritual/aesthetic compartment must yield to the realities of the physical universe. Some scientists would have us believe that their way of thinking is the only way. They suggest that all who hold religious beliefs lead lives of delusion and fantasy at odds with the truths of the cosmos. No doubt the scientific community would be pleased if someday all religious sentiment were supplanted by scientific materialism. If that should happen I wonder if human life would be better.

Much of human activity and thought lies in the subjective domain entirely unverifiable in materialistic terms. Putting the question of God aside, humans hold intimations of beauty and other qualities that science hopes to explain in entirely materialistic terms. Do we love someone because of the beauty of his or her soul or is it just a biochemical imperative? Does the appreciation of a work of art rest on transcendent principles or only on complex neural excitation that gives the illusion of other worldliness? Do our moral impulses stem from a prime giver of the law or are they simply the expression of practical accommodations to current realities? We live, we die and are no more says the scientific materialist. The faces of friends and loved ones are no more than traces in the sand blown away by the winds of time. The scientist might also say, "What difference does it make?" The difference has to do with the idea there are two compartments in the human psyche, as previously asserted.

Thus, an individual lives with two separate but interconnected mind compartments, the materialistic and the spiritual/aesthetic. The spiritual/aesthetic compartment deals in myths and symbols reaching beyond concrete life into the mysterious world of God. I said earlier that the materialistic compartment can inform the spiritual/aesthetic compartment such as was done by Galileo and the geocentric dogma of the universe. Here we see this dogma had really nothing to do with essential precepts of Christ but rather with the faulty perceptions of the physical universe by church hierarchy. However, belief in the geocentric dogma was considered by the clergy to be essential to belief in the church in general and represented the arbitrary assertion of power by the clergy over the masses. Denial of the theory injured only the clergy and not the essential precepts of Christianity. I doubt any members of the clergy today would say that Galileo was wrong in his assertions or that the church was ultimately damaged by them. This is an example of how the materialistic compartment can inform the spiritual/aesthetic compartment and still not exclude it.

What then should we say concerning the miracles associated with Christ and in particular about the resurrection? Should this be considered another arbitrary fable concocted by the clerical hierarchy? Would the Christian Church be harmed by demythologizing the resurrection or would that be similar to debunking the geocentric theory? I think there is a vast difference in the consequences of the two issues. As I intimated at the outset, resurrection is a key principle of the Christian Church whereas geocentricity was not essential to the foundations of the Church. I think Paul was right about the resurrection and its meaning. If Christ had simply died like any person and remained dead it is doubtful the Church would have survived almost 2000 years. He would have been just another mesmerizing cult personality with a limited following. There is a need of the spiritual/aesthetic compartment to incorporate symbols and myths to approach God. It cannot be done with ordinary language.

In this context Paul Tillich has something pertinent to say. He writes: "A myth which is understood as a myth, but not removed or replaced, can be called a 'broken myth'." He felt it was essential to retain broken myths because they are the language of faith. I think this is different from the thinking of those who would demythologize and discard. Tillich in effect, tacitly recognizes the apparent ambiguity of holding belief and disbelief on the same question but finds the paradox essential. The symbolism is essential for the spiritual/ aesthetic compartment to maintain its religious sentiment. Religious sentiment I define as the sense held by a conscious individual standing before God. Understanding the myth as myth allows the "thinking person" to bridge the differences between the current understanding of physical reality afforded by science and the transcendental importance and values of religious sentiment. Although I may not believe in the physical reality of resurrection or the virgin birth in one compartment of my mind I can confess them from the other compartment without reservation. It is not dissimilar to viewing an allegorical painting. The physical appearance of the subjects and themes of the action may seem exaggerated and overdrawn to the point of comedy but the totality of the picture imparts important meaning. The elements of the painting taken individually and out of context may seem trite and without value. Considered as a whole all elements conspire to create a powerful myth.

What I have said thus far concerning the implied importance of religious sentiment is directed to those who are struggling to maintain their faith in the face of post modern criticism. In other words, it is directed to those who are still open to the possibility of God. To those materialists who discount the need or possibility of God, I bid you farewell from this discussion.

In approaching the question of Christ's resurrection I will take a path close to that of Paul Tillich who espouses the "broken myth." I am unable to take the fideistic way that denies a role for human reason in pursuit of religious truth. It is not my intent to proselytize those with established beliefs. It is for those who are searching for a way to fit their wavering faith into a modern context that dismisses the miraculous events inherent in Christianity. I take the miracles to be symbols of religious discourse as meaningful as any symbol used in human discourse. To attribute a rational explanation to a certain myth does not destroy its symbolic meaning and importance. The explanation is formulated in the materialistic mind compartment and the symbol of the explained event is held in the spiritual/aesthetic compartment. This is how I see Tillich's broken myth.

I wholly subscribe to the assertion of the Apostle Paul of the supreme importance of the resurrection to the Christian Faith. Paul was not asserting a Hellenistic spiritual resurrection but one of the body, a corporeal resurrection. Christ's physical body was needed to impress witnesses that God was serious and that Christ was truly discharging the mandate he was given by God. How many heroes had already died whose souls had gone to heaven but their corruptible bodies remained quiet in the grave? The living body of Christ was necessary to make a point that God was involved in the physical world, the Kingdom of God on Earth.

Here we must digress for a while to consider how God might intervene in the physical world. Scientific materialists ridicule the notion of a divine creator who is actively engaged in creation. Prayer is considered an absurdity. I personally do not believe that God interdicts or changes the natural laws He created to intervene in human affairs. A patient with an incurable disease is not rescued by changing the physical events that caused the disease but by the timely application of a treatment that could reverse or alter those etiologic forces. It is just possible that God's subliminal prompting of the therapist and guidance of treatment might be operative. There is no magical suspension of the rules. In addition the patient's mind could be directed to a source of treatment and given the willingness to accept it and to maintain a positive frame of mind. I see God's will carried out by his people working in the physical world under divine instigation and inspiration. It is by myths and metaphors we are prompted to do God's work.

Returning to the issue of Christ's resurrection, how can the event be analyzed from the perspective of materialistic realities and still maintain its important mythical significance? Historical context is critical. The concept of resurrection had a number of meanings and implications to the Jews at the time of Christ, the so-called second temple Jews. To the Jews of the Babylonian captivity, resurrection symbolized freedom from oppression, the triumph of the Jehovah's people and the re-establishment of Israel. It was a cipher for a nation, not for the individual. The Pharisees believed there would ultimately be an embodied resurrection of the righteous at some future time, a notion completely rejected by the Sadducees. The Sadducees asserted that the current life was all there was so one had better enjoy it. A spiritual non-corporeal resurrection was a legacy of Greek Hellenistic philosophy widely held in the Jewish community. An immediate corporeal resurrection after physical death was something most Jews had difficulty accepting. So there was a variety of interpretations of the meaning of resurrection. To Paul the resurrection had to be physical or Christian faith was in vain. A considerable body of modern Christian scholars holds the bodily resurrection to be an historical fact in support of the Pauline claim. But why is the distinction between a spiritual versus a bodily resurrection so important and what can be said 2000 years after the event that makes sense to the modern mind tempered by scientific materialism? Is it possible an examination of conditions and customs existing 2000 years ago can provide an understanding of the putative event that makes both spiritual and material sense? If that is possible, we are creating, thereby, a Tillichian "broken myth", one we can retain for our discourse with God. I believe we can.

Historical evidence supports the view that something unique and special happened on Easter Sunday. I assert that something special had to be the physical resurrection of Jesus of Nazareth. What immense meaning the physical resurrection had to have. This was not simply an illusion, a Hellenistic rising of a spirit but a tangible indication that henceforth the world would be different. God was keeping the promise He made through the person of Jesus Christ.

A number of theories of the resurrection can be cited that question the physical validity of the resurrection story. They include outright fraud perpetrated by the disciples or other interested persons who could have stolen the body. Hugh J. Schonfield in his book, "The Passover Plot", suggests that Christ deliberately scripted and orchestrated the entire passion story with the aid of other conspirators possibly including Joseph of Arimathea in whose tomb Christ was interred. He goes on to say that while on the cross Jesus was drugged to create the appearance of death. In the tomb he recovered from the potion and emerged to meet his disciples. The physical encounter was a necessary transforming sign that galvanized the disciples to propagate Christ's message and thereby create the Christian Church. Schonfield's theory, as well as those presupposing the theft of a physically dead body, all requires deception and fraud perpetrated not only by friends and disciples but by Jesus as well. To accept any of these theories requires a fundamental distrust of the legitimacy and verity of the person of Christ and his mission. Fraud and deception are wholly inconsistent with the Christian message and I personally reject such theories.

Two facts stand out that lend credence to the theory I am about to propose. First, Christ's legs were not broken as was the custom. Second, his time in the tomb was of relatively short duration, probably less than 48 hours. To me this means he may not have been, by modern standards, physiologically dead. Had his legs been broken he surely would have died due to massive hemorrhage compounding the other elements of crucifixion. Furthermore, had he survived with legs broken, he could not have walked and made appearances for 40 days. (I am of course making these arguments in purely materialistic terms.) It has been calculated that the duration on the cross was probably in the order of three hours. While any time must have been a horrifying experience it is still of a brevity that could favor a near death outcome.

Secondly, his short residence in the tomb is consistent with a near death experience. It was customary for the Jews to visit tombs on the third day to make sure the body was actually dead. This was considered a sound interval to differentiate the truly dead from the apparently dead. Beyond three days there was little chance of making a mistake.

What were the criteria for death used 2000 years ago? Obviously we cannot be sure. The chief criterion probably was the decision of the person in charge of the execution. It can only be imagined how thoroughly corpses were checked in the ghoulish excitement and probable chaos of a multiple crucifixion. Clearly no sophisticated tests could be used such as an electrocardiogram or an electroencephalogram to be absolutely sure. Near or apparent death was and is not unusual. History is replete with such stories. Breathing can be so shallow and pulse so weak as to be undetectable to the unaided observer. The custom of the Jews 2000 years ago to double check the status of the corpse after three days attests to this reality. In the 19th century a French physician reported 162 cases of "apparent death" seven of whom recovered in from 36 to 42 hours after death was pronounced. Thus, it is quite within the bounds of possibility that Christ was taken down from the cross and placed in the tomb of Joseph of Arimathea in a near death state. Yet, all who saw the body considered it dead. Thus, it *was* dead. Criteria of the times were apparently met as is clearly stated in the scriptures.

Alone in the tomb Christ recovers consciousness. His last recollection was terrible pain and fading senses on the cross.

Now He feels alive. Can He be dreaming? No, He *is* alive. Lying on a stone slab in the tomb He feels the cold surface, He feels the pain of His wounds all signaling that once again He is a sentient being. What He has taught and what He believes has come to pass. He has been raised from the dead by his Heavenly Father.

This scenario incorporates no deception or fraud by any party to the event. It adheres to the scriptural record. What objections can be raised? Some would say that the body must have been truly dead to fulfill the scriptures. I would again ask, what were the criteria for death at that time? If the critics insist on a body that has putrefied to come back to real life there are inherent contradictions in their argument. Invoking a putrefied body is invoking a materialistic idea. A putrefied body does not reconstitute itself and return to an animated pre-death living state in materialistic experience. It is similar to saying the world is the center of the universe. An apparent death can be reversible. What I am trying to do is de-mythologize, to create the "broken myth" of Tillich. I want to explain the myth but not to discard it. The Resurrection is an irreplaceable part of Christianity. Without the Resurrection there is no Christianity. It is the chief symbol of our relationship to God. It is part of the lexicon we must use in our discourse about and with God. This hypothetical story is genuine—there is no deception.

Once again, I recognize my words will not be well received by many. The fideist will reject any attempt at rational materialistic analysis of spiritual matters. Fair enough. What is important is for the individual person to arrive at his or her own set of views and doctrines that make sense and are consistent with his or her perception of the meaning of life. I would not want to change that. It is a personal choice. For the hard scientific materialist who rejects any concept of a Supreme Being or God I would say the same. Whatever makes you comfortable is fine with me.

I make my appeal to those who are truly open to the idea of God but who cannot accept what they consider to be the rigid literalism of the church. How can they endorse doctrines they consider no more than superstitions wholly outside the realm of rational discourse?

I have suggested there are two distinct although interrelated mind compartments, the materialistic and the spiritual/aesthetic that process information differently. When operating in the materialistic sphere in the course of daily living, cause and effect observations are continuously made. When I turn the key in the ignition in my car the motor starts. When I engage the transmission I expect the car to move. Most of our daily actions and activities are a flow of causes and effects most of which are expected on the basis of previous experience. Why is that dog digging a hole in my yard? What is it after? The search for causes, reasons or explanations is the essence of the conscious cognitive process. Similarly, in the spiritual/aesthetic realm, there is a linear process of what or why but using a different data base. I am conscious. Why was consciousness created and who or what did it? The day is beautiful. Who or what caused it? Or the day is ugly. Why is it so?

To ask is there a God, a first cause, or a prime mover of the universe, is a fundamental question eventually posed to most if not all people. No matter how the question is framed it must be confronted. Is there a God Creator? If so, there must be meaningfulness to life. Or, if the proposition of God is refuted then there is no meaningfulness to life other than that it occurs. Answers to this great question are always a matter of personal choice. We have choice because we are conscious. Those who chose to believe in things not verifiable in the materialistic realm are exercising *faith*.

In the spiritual/aesthetic compartment, ciphers and codes are used that employ symbols and myths. They are the *lingua franca* of this realm. Not only are words and collections of words into stories and myths a part of this language, so are events such as the resurrection. Materialists assert there is only one world, that of physical reality. Spiritual/aestheticists claim there is another reality juxtaposed to physical reality. It is a domain of mystery transcending the physical world. A barrier or thin membrane separates the physical from the transcendent spiritual/aesthetic domain. Symbols and myths are required to pierce that barrier and permit access to a reality that gives life meaningfulness.

The resurrection story is of fundamental importance to the Christian Faith. Paul says that without the resurrection our faith is in vain. His claim is of immense profundity. Many Christians in this modern era of science find their faith flagging because of difficulty reconciling the physical world with what many consider to be superstitions embodied in religious dogma. I contend that the search for God is inherent in the human psyche and will not go away no matter how thoroughly science may define and explain the physical world. It is because we have two mind compartments, the materialistic and the spiritual/aesthetic, each one deals in different ways with the problem of existence. It is possible; indeed it is propitious for the individual to utilize both compartments in approaching life.

In this treatise I have offered the story of Christ's resurrection for examination in the light of Paul Tillich's concept of the broken myth. This examination involves both compartments of the mind that I have described. The materialistic compartment informs the spiritual/aesthetic compartment but does not destroy it. A myth is "broken" but not discarded. Rather, it is used in our discussions about and with God. In this sense we can confess our faith with no sense of hypocrisy or naiveté.

The Interface

Being a Christian implies belief in the historical flesh and blood of Christ who died as well as in the transcendental living Christ who permeates all our earthly experience in present time. It is a problem to get Christ across the interface of physical to spiritual reality. Trying to make sense of the crucifixion, death and resurrection has been a perennial challenge to lay people and theologians alike. As it is impossible to know the exact nature of the transition, all who accept the story do so as a matter of faith. After all, that is what religion is, an accommodation of the unknowable to the present based on conviction without verification, i.e. faith. To the believer the total message of Christ makes such intuitive sense that most or all ambiguities are accepted as true.

Given that faith is an imperative in Christianity, does it make any sense to attempt some rational explanation of the miraculous stories about Christ, in particular His resurrection? Is there any harm caused by attempting to dispel some of the mystery? This is also an old question. Many would say, leave the issue alone; faith can only be weakened where it is not needed. I disagree. I start from the position of completely accepting the Christian message. It is so strong that nothing can shake me from it. But I need at least to attempt to find a possible link between the physical and metaphysical aspects of Christ. Whereas I realize that to discuss religion in terms of physical laws may be inappropriate, the discussion of the interface between the physical and spiritual can provide the basis of an even firmer religious faith.

The death and resurrection provides a poignant focus for this discussion. A literal interpretation leads to some absurd possibilities. If Christ was reconstituted as a real physical being and is living among us, subject to all the physicals laws of his age, He would be 2000 years old and likely in a most decrepit state. Moreover, where does He reside? Who supplies his food and other sustenance? Surely someone must see Him and be able to report on Him.

But you will counter, He is no longer on earth but in heaven with God the Father. If his physical body was transported where did it go, up, down, out one million miles to some remote celestial body? Quite obviously we cannot rationally accept a physical resurrection and current presence of Christ. We are talking about a spiritual being, not subject to physical laws.

How can we reconcile the Biblical account? How could we explain the record of apparent coming back to life and then ostensibly disappearing into thin air to be with God? Schonfield, in his book <u>The Passover Plot</u> suggests that Christ, when taken down from the cross, was in an inanimate state simulating death due to a potion he was given. Thus, his physical resurrection appeared real as He became reanimated from the death-like sleep. What happened after His brief post resurrection sojourn on earth? Could he possibly have wandered off into the wilderness, dying of natural causes? If so His physical body could have decayed or been consumed leaving no earthly trace? It seems to me all these possibilities can still leave us with an unsullied Christ. This construction is simply an attempt to elucidate possible metaphorical mechanisms that can aid our human understanding of the closeness of physical to metaphysical realities.

The following illustration is offered in support of the assertion that our metaphysical nature is more imminent than we are consciously aware. It is said by scientists that our physical bodies turn over approximately every seven years. That is to say all molecules in our bodies are exchanged (with the possible exception of bone which has a longer turnover period) gradually over seven years, in a real sense, we are new people. Still we are recognized as the same old person by our friends and family. Our personalities just have a new house or facade. Similarly, any physical structure could theoretically undergo a similar transformation. For example, all the bricks in a brick building could be sequentially and gradually replaced to imperceptibly create a new structure without affecting its appearance. Or an automobile could undergo a complete renewal without altering its original features. What is important is the maintenance of the original personality, structure or function rather than the original physical building blocks. Though the physical structures disappear, their plans remain. In reality we are abstract plan or idea rendered in physical materials. Even our genes are physically mutable by the turn over of its component DNA but the blueprint persists.

By this argument it is apparent that intangible, non-palpable plan, idea or concept, i.e. the metaphysical element in our reality, subordinates our physical substance. Whether we are conscious of it or not, we live at once in both the physical and metaphysical worlds. When Christ crossed the interface from the physical to the metaphysical world he was simply shucking the husk of humanity to reveal the mystical seed that was and is of primary importance. Certainly we will all do the same some day. How this may have occurred in physical terms in no way disquiets me. In fact it strengthens me and makes me more aware of the mystery of my existence each day.

I would seek no conclusive earthly explanation for religious faith although there is a large body of empirical evidence for its validity. Faith will only be unnecessary when we are face to face with our creator. However, we should not discard our intellects in approaching the question of faith. In the physical world there are abundant clues to the mystery of our being and to the soundness of faith.

The Temple of the Spirit

(A homily given at Christ Chapel, Gustavus Adolphus
College February 13, 1978)

Chaplain Elvee, Fellow Gustavians:

This fall will be twenty four years since I last spoke in Chapel.
The long interval may suggest I am in great demand as a
speaker and hence, you are the recipients of a rare opportunity. Alternatively, there is little demand for my oratorical
talents leaving you this morning as captives of a bold novice.
You will decide. Instead of hearing from a man of the cloth,
this morning you will hear from a man of the bandage which
will, at least, be a change.

My last twenty two years have been spent in medicine. When I
started out I envisioned bastions of disease collapsing before
the onslaught of my burning youthful sword. I was to extend
life, to relieve suffering, to improve the human condition. My
enthusiasm led me to believe it would be easy. Now, with these
years behind me I feel as though I am attempting to catch
a waterfall with a cup. My perception of the role of a physician has changed. My new perception is not cynical. Rather,
I would like to think it is a clearer more realistic view of what
the meaning of life is and what our collective mission is.

We are taught there are certain aspects of life to beware lest
they prevent us from the realization of a full and happy life.
I am talking about such things as preoccupation with material wealth and power. One does not have to look far to

find examples of all the unhappiness wrought by such preoccupation. At Gustavus we are admonished to first seek the kingdom of God and all other things will be added or fall in place. The transcendental truth of this admonition looms ever larger in my mind.

Of all the obstacles to spiritual development there is one which has not gained much notice and I am speaking about preoccupation with our physical health. Paul, in his letter to the Corinthians refers to the body as the temple of the Holy Spirit imparting a sacred quality to the flesh. Indeed, we are taught that all is God's creation requiring a respectful recognition. There is a popular cliché, "if you have your health you have everything." Twenty years ago I would have said amen; now I'm not so sure.

Daily I see bodies beautiful as Greek statues that contain wretched spirits. I also see bodies torn and aching with disease that possess glorious, burning, beautiful spirits, more lovely than any work of human art. Conversely, some have both beautiful bodies and spirits and some have wretched bodies and wretched spirits. The common denominator is obviously the quality of the spirit that gives life its meaning.

We are constantly deluged with propaganda from the media, our friends and colleagues and our parents admonishing us to preserve and husband our bodies.; don't miss meals, put on your galoshes, get plenty of rest, exercise, don't worry, don't work too hard etc. The tacit promise is if one adheres to these rituals life will be better. To put it another way, you'll be healthy, wealthy and wise. My experience suggests it is not so.

The western world and the United States in particular are too preoccupied with physical health similar to our preoccupation with the gathering and storing of the world's goods. We have been duped that modern scientific medicine can alter our destinies and give us something to make us feel better. We can also help ourselves by not drinking alcohol, not smoking, staying lean, jogging regularly. It's an illusion. The waterfall is too big for the cup. To the degree we are preoccupied with our bodies, to that degree we are detracted from our attention of our spiritual health.

Reasonable attention to our health is good but our health rituals should not delude us. Jogging can be fun, even a spiritual experience but if done solely on the hope it will extend life, forget it. The same can be said for the other prescriptions and proscriptions mentioned.

Rather than a temple I would chose to compare the body to a vehicle, a vehicle of the spirit. It should not rest indolently on some acropolis. Rather, it should carry us about the world, exposing us to an infinite variety of experience from which we can gain a greater knowledge of God's purpose for us.

Our bodies are our automobiles. We may chose to pamper them, polish them, bring them often to the garage and rarely if ever take them on the dusty rough roads of life. They will look good but they won't do any good or provide any adventure. Alternatively we can periodically put gas and oil in them and drive them everywhere. Occasionally there may be a knock or lurch requiring a mechanic's attention. But don't wait to get back on the highway as soon as possible. Let it burn out not rust out.

There is a relevant analogy between a successful athlete and life in general. In order to succeed the athlete must endure pain, play in spite of injury, and play hurt as it were. Let us all place more attention on our spiritual health; let our bodies be the servants of our spirits.

There is a degree of urgency about this matter. I am convinced that by the end of college our essential patterns of thought and behavior are practically set. Any significant changes are to be made by tremendous releases of energy often occasioned by cataclysmic occurrences. The time is now.

Time and Happiness

(A homily given at Christ Chapel Gustavus Adolphus
College December 1983)

A few weeks ago as I began preparing my thoughts for this
homily I decided to begin with the old phrase, "eat, drink
and be merry for tomorrow you die." I reached this decision
without foreknowledge of today's scripture lesson. When informed we would be reading I Corinthians 15:12-34 which
contains the phrase, "eat drink and be merry for tomorrow
we die," I was struck by the coincidence. I shall not waste
words attempting to decide if this was pure chance or a mysterious foreordained act of divine providence.

This lesson brings to our thoughts considerations of time,
particularly the present and how it may be affected by our anticipation of the future. Paul uses the "eat and drink" phrase
in a pejorative sense as an expression of the hopeless exploi-
tation of pleasure today in absence of hope for the morrow.
We know Christ was indeed raised and, therefore we need
not concern ourselves with such base activity.

I fear, however, that as Christians with a transcendental
promise of resurrection in the future we live too much in
the future and pay not enough heed to the present. I do not
believe that was Christ's intention. As humans we are woven
in a fabric of time and space the chief dimension of which
is the present. I contend that life is to be enjoyed not simply

endured and I further believe that Christ came to facilitate our happiness not to defer it.

Twenty five years in medicine have afforded me the opportunity to study and appraise human behavior. In that time many people have come under my care and I have intimately shared much joy and sorrow with them. Undoubtedly external events and forces have a bearing on ones outlook on life and state of happiness. Even the most buoyant and resilient personalities can be crushed, at least temporarily, by circumstances. Conversely I have seen those glum individuals who will not be cheered even by the most pleasant and favorable event that might occur in their favor. It is clear to me that internal forces and resources of the individual that determine happiness not the external ones.

What are the characteristics of happy people? What are their unique internal forces and resources? The first characteristic I would cite is will, the will to be happy. Happy people make the choice to be happy. Reality is a mix of good and bad as it has always been and will always be. It is incumbent upon the happy person to choose the good as his or her preoccupation. There is so much good in the world if only we will see it. Look around, look inside; you have youth, intelligence, sunshine, trees, that pretty loving girl, the handsome faithful boy, your friends, music; all of it permeates our existence if only you make the choice to be conscious of it. Cynicism should find no room in your thoughts.

The second characteristic of happy people is courage to meet reality head on. True happiness is not to be found in flight from reality. The daily task must be discharged; work is not put off; success is celebrated; failure is faced. In other words, there is courage for the day.

These qualities of will and courage have the dimension of time and that time is the present, the now. Do candles burn in the past? No, only their memory. Do candles burn in the future? We do not know but we hope so. Candles burn now; we see their shine and feel their warmth now. So it is with happiness.

Gustavus Adolphus College is an excellent example of the tripartite time. Futurism is in great abundance here; you are all working hard for your futures. We are also aware of the great past and traditions of this dear institution. However, we must not be preoccupied with either the past or the future lest we miss this day and fail to savor it.

Some of you here today may not have the gift of happiness. If you don't you must practice. You must not say that if such and such a thing happens of a favorable nature I will then be happy. NO. You must say, today I seek happiness. If you muster the forces of happiness and develop the will and courage they require you will live nobly and your present will be fulfilling. When you become confident of this day there should be no fear of tomorrow and your yesterdays will be a glowing testimony to your todays.

We of all people who have heard liberating messages in this holy place should be particularly well-equipped to live today in happiness and confidence because we have the assurance that God is with us. So then, let us all eat, drink and be merry; let us study, work, love and be happy **today** for tomorrow we live.

A Letter to Esby on Prayer

Dear Esby:

I am somewhat apprehensive to write on the subject of prayer to a great theologian and thinker such as you. Nonetheless, I will do so.

I like the simple definition of prayer found in Webster's dictionary: "to address God with adoration, confession, supplication or thanksgiving." To address God is an act of faith that there is a God, that He (or She … I'd prefer not to get into that tortuous distinction of gender so I will continue in the masculine) is receptive to us and is disposed to respond to our prayers. Furthermore, prayer is essentially a <u>conscious act</u> wherein we are aware of what we are saying to God. Is it possible our unconscious minds pray? I don't know how we can apprehend this possibility so it must remain moot. Quite likely our subconscious mind continually processes thoughts and feeds them upward into consciousness but it is the conscious state that is the final arbiter of the content. In the conscious state we can weigh choices deliberately. Consciousness enables free will or choice (if in fact we have them). Consciousness is required for moral decisions.

Prayer is a conscious recognition of the primacy of God in our lives. Prayer is our umbilical cord to God. It defines a relationship and solidarity with God similar to children and parents maintaining their affection for one another. The most important element is our striving to have a relationship with God as represented by our prayer efforts. Having established this relationship it is hard for me to imagine how considerations of quantity or quality of prayer have any meaning. God can't be bribed. He will not suspend the natural law He created simply to relieve our suffering. If we stand in awe of the Creator and have trust in Him we must view everything as gift, even the bad.

I am reminded of the physician who comes into the hospital room of a severely ill patient. The air is filled with alarm and dread. The patient and onlookers are in anguish. The physician calms the air and stills the alarm with the coolness and authority administered with compassion. Perhaps the final outcome is not affected by his demeanor but the anxiety and mental pain have been mollified. In our prayers we ought to seek the coolness and grace of God. We may wish for altered outcomes for our dilemmas and that may or may not be realized but we should always ask for courage to withstand all of life's challenges. The most important petition is for the maintenance of our faith in God.

How does God intervene in the world? Does He use magic tricks? There is obviously much mystery in the manner in which the Creator intercedes in man's affairs. Undoubtedly, God uses us to effect the petitions of our prayers. In this sense it is appropriate to break down prayer into private and public.

In our private prayers, God can help us sort out our thoughts to find solutions we are able to achieve with our own resources. God serves as counselor infusing us with knowledge and insights that can result in positive conscious action.

In public prayer a broad spectrum of people are exposed to petitions and may be galvanized to respond to them. We the people must be a major reservoir of God's agents for action on prayer. God knows our thoughts and desires so that any verbalization of prayer must be meant for the attention of the hearers. When we petition out loud we are hoping others will hear and come to our aid.

So, my dear friend and mentor, those are my random thoughts about prayer at this time in my life. Maybe they will change. I always prefer to discuss such matters face to face whenever that opportunity may arise.

PART FIVE

On Art And Artists

The Uncircumcised David

I saw Michelangelo's statue of David for the first time in 1954. I had sought out the *Accademia di Belle Arti* in Florence while studying in Europe as a 20 year old undergraduate. To see David was a major quest fueled by the stories I had read about him in my studies. My first view of the huge statue was impressive. First I stood at a distance with a sense of reverence. What I had read did not prepare me for the moment nor even begin to capture the eloquence, grandeur and nobility of the figure.

Coming closer I began to appreciate the detail of muscles, veins, fingernails and hair. One disconcerting feature was the apparent disproportion of the head and hands to the rest of the body. They seemed larger than they ought to be. Was the disproportion real? If so was it intended or was it inadvertent? I subsequently made measurements from photographs and determined they were indeed oversized.

It would be 24 years before I saw David again. In 1978 I took my wife for her first visit to Florence. As an artist herself, she devoured Florentine art and like me, she was deeply impressed by David. We must have spent more than an hour looking at the statue from different angles. It was as though we were trying to extract every possible thought and experience for fear of not returning. It was intense. We peered, cocked our heads, stepped back and stepped forward.

Then I became aware of a detail that escaped me 24 years before. I called it to my wife's attention. David, the quintessential Jew, was not circumcised! "What do you think that means?" I asked. She looked at me with a smile and shook her head.

We left the Belle Arti with unsure feelings one might experience having been deluged with so much sensory input. We sorted some of it out over dark shots of espresso in a nearby café. The disproportion of head and hands was now augmented by the lack of circumcision further increasing the enigma of David. My curiosity remained unresolved. The issue would rest for the time being.

Another twelve years passed before my next encounter with David. This time we were in the company of another couple, two good friends who were also art conscious. "Notice the large head and hands," I said trying to act the role of a docent. "Now, look closely at the penis. Why do you think he was not circumcised?" No one offered an opinion but my wife cast a somewhat hopeless look as though she were trying to persuade her child to stop bathroom talk.

The reader may think my preoccupation with David's uncircumcised penis exposes some morbid sexual obsession. Not so. Although this minute observation seems insignificant I feel it is pregnant with meaning. For years it recurred in my idle thoughts but I could not come to a satisfactory explanation from my own fund of knowledge. I would need to do some research. This is the synthesis of that research. It is necessary to consider not only the penis but the aforementioned disproportions of the head and hands to give a total context of meaning.

First, consider the large head and hands. It is naïve to think this was not intended given the genius of Michelangelo. I read somewhere he did this to preserve apparent body proportions when viewed from below. There is another possibility that would fulfill an esthetic intent. The large hands give accent to what David did with his hands, namely fling the stone that killed the giant, Goliath. David was the righteous underdog who prevailed. The head, i.e. the mind of David, gives the statue its prime artistic metaphor. The face, a mirror to the mind, is defiant and resolute, radiating immense character. Although the torso is beautiful in its own right, it is subservient to the head and hands. There is the look of Apollo about David. Not only is he Hebrew, he is also Greek, personifying a Platonic world of ideals in a heroic figure. The melding of Greek and Hebrew produces a universal. David is at once worldly mortal and ineffable spirit.

How does circumcision fit into this analysis? At the time of Michelangelo, circumcision was confined to the Jews and Arabs. The rest of manhood was uncircumcised. It is apparent from Greek statuary that Greek men were also uncircumcised. Thus, for David to join the ranks of universal man he could not bear the distinctive mark of a specific tribe. He could not be circumcised.

When I next see David I will look on him with new insights. No longer will I harbor doubts about Michelangelo's artistic intentions. I will see David with big effective hands governed by a noble mind and spirit. Inspired by Hebraic and Greek conceptions, he belongs to everyone.

Music My Love

Music has been an essential part of my life since childhood. My father whistled and sang. Either I adopted his ways by imitation or we had common genes for those talents. My vocal abilities first came to public attention at about age 12 when I was permitted to join the church choir. Without prior warning the director pointed at me to sing the solo in, "I Wonder as I Wander." I executed it with ease and a beauty that surprised even me. From that time forward I was given many opportunities to sing before many different audiences. I became soloist for the high school choir; I had the leading role in an opera. Continuing in college I was a frequent soloist with the college choir.

There were other early influences in my developing passion for music. My music teacher in primary school was a beautiful red-haired lady whom I adored. She was an excellent pianist who gathered us around the piano to sing songs and hear her play. Frequently she gave hugs so that music became identified with warmth and affection. I also had a much-loved aunt who introduced me to the waltzes of Strauss and other light classics by way of her collection of 78 RPM records. Thus, I was entwined by a number of musical roots that grounded my affinity for tempo, tone and texture.

I came to love most forms of music but I most favor classical and Jazz, not an unusual combination. Hard rock may cause me to tap my feet but I confess to difficulty in finding much pleasure in it.

Now, at age 68, an extensive musical history lies behind me. I have attended concerts by the Minnesota Orchestra-formerly called the Minneapolis Symphony-for almost fifty years. I have seen many operas in some of the finest houses of the world in New York, Munich, Vienna, Berlin, Prague and Hamburg. Many great conductors and soloists have entertained me in live performances. My collection of recordings beginning with vinyl LP's and now compact discs have proliferated to the point there is no longer sufficient time to hear them all again.

Given technological advances it would not surprise me if an entire Wagnerian opera will someday fit on a disc no larger than a quarter. Technology has allowed a wide dissemination of music to all corners of the world and even to space. It has been said that, because of recordings, more people now hear Bach's music in one day than all who ever heard it during his life time. No doubt electronics are a boon to all music aficionados. Nevertheless, I prefer live performances preferably in a building with good acoustics.

It occurs to me on many occasions while clapping my hands red for a fantastic performance that for hundreds of years countless music lovers have experienced similar thrilling moments of acoustical, visual and social pleasure afforded by concert halls and opera stages. Aside from requirements of illumination, there is no need for electronic enhancements. The wonderful sounds that enthrall me at Orchestra Hall in Minneapolis work similar magic in patrons in similar venues around the world as for instance at the *Musikverein* in Vienna. Acoustical engineers have analyzed and characterized the qualities of great halls and have had success in recreating them in new structures to ensure the potential for exciting live performances. It is the unadorned live classical musical performance in a great facility I seek out to experience a sense of solidarity with enthusiasts in all parts of the globe and throughout history. When I think about it, I am awed and in love.

A Cigar for Biederman

My home town, Red Wing, Minnesota, has only a few distinctions that would attract the attention of the outside world. One of those distinctions is that it is the home of a world class artist, Charles Biederman. He may not be well known to the average American, but to the world art community he is one of the contemporary giants.

Recently an extensive article on the artist appeared in the Minneapolis Star Tribune. It chronicled times from his birth in 1906 in Cleveland, Ohio, to his early education, and his study in Paris where he met Leger, Miro and Modrian among others. In 1942 he moved to Red Wing where he has lived and worked ever since. The article went on to tell of the eleven books he has written and the large collection of his works bequeathed to the Frederick R. Weisman Art Museum on the campus of the University of Minnesota. Since the death of his wife in 1975, he has lived alone in a modest old house in a wooded area where he walks daily and takes inspiration. At age 92 he continues to create.

It is my thought that an artist who is still mentally competent at such an extreme age ought to have few if any fears of life, which brings me to the crux of this tale. The newspaper article revealed he had "chain smoked cigars" for more than 50 years but that he had recently quit on the advice of a Mayo Clinic doctor. When I read that I thought I would jump up and down with amazement and anger. Stop smoking cigars at age 92?! What in the world could have led to this ridiculous decision?

Obviously two people were involved, at least in the first discussion with his physician. Perhaps Biederman wanted to quit for some undisclosed reason but then, it seems to me, he would have done it on his own. If he already had some serious disease as a consequence of smoking, it is unlikely that stopping at this late date would have had any measurable effect on the out come. Maybe he hated cigars although that seems unlikely given his long-standing habit. Moreover, it is not unheard of to enjoy smoking. It has many positive rewards for the psyche. It would not surprise me at all if the artist admitted that cigars were important in sustaining the creative impulse. So I would suggest that Biederman enjoyed his cigars and was reluctant to separate himself from them.

Thus, I see the nefarious doctor as the perpetrator of this outrage. I considered him a self-righteous medical zealot, out to rid the world of tobacco. He would claim that tobacco is bad. It should not be used in any situation. Damn those Indians who first sold it to the explorers. May they all rot in hell. It is bad, bad, bad. I can't even stand to be with anyone who smokes. It is disgusting. You would think people had more sense.

How do I know the mind of this type? As a lung specialist I worked with such people for over 40 years. I know whereof I speak. This posture typifies a trend in medicine that has increased over the past twenty years. With increasing scientific and technologic advances the individual has become less an individual and more a part of a cohort of specific diseases. The disease has become the point of interest, not the patient. The disease must be treated, not the patient. Perhaps I am exaggerating a bit but I do so to emphasize the shift that has occurred in the doctor-patient relationship. It is not good.

The syllogism is as follows: Tobacco can cause disease, by avoiding smoking, these diseases are preventable; therefore, it is incumbent upon the physician to stop the use of tobacco—not entirely unreasonable. There are, however, some facts to take into consideration. Does tobacco cause disease in all users? No, it does not, at least in any readily measurable way. By avoiding smoking, the diseases associated with smoking will not develop. Unfortunately, whereas the incidence of these diseases may be less, they will still occur in non-smokers.

Does tobacco provide any positive effects? Indeed it does. Even if there were deleterious effects from tobacco, is there a period of use that seals the user's fate making interdiction futile? Most likely there is. Should the positive effects be weighed against the negative effects? Of course they should. A mentally competent artist–or a person of any occupation—who has acceded to 92 years ought to be allowed a few terminal pleasures. Having heard the intolerant preaching about tobacco from many colleagues, particularly in recent times, I am not surprised by the Biederman story, only disappointed by the lack of maturity and humaneness in the physician's advice.

What is even more astonishing is that Biederman apparently took the advice or maybe he really hasn't. He may be in the closet and takes a few drags when no one is looking. I doubt he would get away with that because the doctor would smell smoke on his breath or on his clothing or may even surreptitiously check his urine for the by products of nicotine to insure compliance. These hard-nose doctors will do anything to save the world from disease.

Let us postulate that Biederman really did stop smoking. The question returns, why does a 92 year old artist of world renown, who has seen so much of life, measured its uncertainties, and experienced its ironies accept the naïve, although scientifically grounded, advice of this physician? Perhaps the physician is an authority figure that Biederman respects or is compelled to respect out of some deep subliminal inclination created by an early developmental trauma. It is strange that an artist who broke so many artistic barriers and defied authority should have second thoughts at brushing aside any authority he did not respect. It doesn't fit.

Could it be he stopped smoking to expiate a sense of guilt? Over what God knows. The newspaper article notes that the art pieces donated to the Weisman Museum reeked of tobacco necessitating a thorough cleaning. Thus, the curator could have been in league with the physician in promoting the anti-smoking campaign to avoid further cleanups. A niece of Biederman once observed him in his studio surrounded by butterflies that were attracted to his cigar smoke. Maybe Biederman wanted to avoid butterflies.

So our gallant physician must swell with pride over his conquest of the great artist. What a sense of power the noble interdiction must render. Before the hubris becomes too large the possible downside must be considered.

Some years ago, I attended a man who wrote scripts for a popular television comedy. He told me he was most productive when sitting in his favorite San Francisco café drinking coffee and smoking cigarettes in endless chains. He tried it without cigarettes but his muse left him. Consequently he moved to another state finding a new haven where smoking was permitted. He was back in business.

The writer was in his mid forties. Although he consumed 40 cigarettes daily, my tests revealed no damage. What should he do? He knew smoking would probably eventually harm his physical health. I asked him if he really wanted to stop smoking. With force and conviction he said, no. He expressed his concern and guilt about abusing his body but he was equally concerned he would dry up professionally if he did not have his cigarettes. "Writing is my whole life," he said. "I don't do it for money; I simply love it; I can't help it." This made sense to me.

After a thorough discussion of the risks for cancer, emphysema and other links with smoking, I told him the decision to stop was his alone. I informed him of various pharmacological and psychological aids but told him the decision must finally be his. No one can or ought to force him. Certainly I would not. Was smoking really essential to the quality of his life, I asked. Thoughtfully he nodded yes. So, I shook his hand and bid him farewell. He grasped my hand and flashed a broad smile signaling relief and gratitude.

Was smoke a catalyst for Biederman's art? I suspect it was. His physician should have given him reassurance not proscription. I would have told him to go on smoking. If I had insisted he stop smoking and he complied I would have to endure the regrettable possibility I helped to blunt the expression of his creative urges or closed the door on them completely. I could tolerate the knowledge he would not reach 100 years or even 93 if he continued smoking as long as he continued creating and attracting butterflies. Therefore, I say, a cigar for Biederman!

A Cigar for Biederman: The Sequel

After I wrote the story on Biederman I considered sending it to him for comment. I didn't for a number of reasons. First, he was such an imposing figure in my mind that I thought he might consider my efforts sophomoric, not worthy of his attention. Such a rejection I did not want to risk. Second, as I was trying to analyze his private psyche he might have been insulted. Lastly, I have always had respect for the privacy of celebrities and my article may have seemed intrusive. Thus, my story lay dormant for over four years.

In late December 2002 a short article appeared in the Minneapolis Sunday paper announcing an open house and exhibition at the Anderson Center for Interdisciplinary Studies in Red Wing. It said that original paintings by such masters as Picasso, and Matisse as well as other notables would be on display. This attraction galvanized our decision to drive to Red Wing on a late December Saturday afternoon.

The Anderson Estate is a few miles north of Red Wing proper. I had passed it hundreds of times but never ventured on the grounds. My mother told me she spent some over-nights there as a child because one of the Anderson children had been a school friend. A. P. Anderson, or as he was commonly called Millionaire Anderson, had made his fortune by inventing puffed wheat and puffed rice. After his death his heirs established the Anderson Center. No doubt the arts orientation was due to the fact that John Anderson, the son, was an accomplished artist. John was also the husband of

Eugenie Anderson who was prominent in Minnesota politics and once served as American Ambassador to Denmark. Her sister, Mary, would become Biederman's wife.

On entering the Anderson Center We encountered a man whose name tag read Robert Hedin. I introduced myself and asked him if he were related to the late and well-known Red Wing surgeon, Raymond Hedin. He said he was his son. Immediately our conversation turned to common experiences and people in Red Wing. It was his mother, Millionaire Anderson's daughter who was my late mother's school friend. I asked about his mother. Pointing over my shoulder he said, "There she is." Turning around I went a few steps and introduced myself to the smiling lady who although near 90 appeared vigorous and enthusiastic. She did not remember my face but she lit up as she heard my name. Her husband had been one of my icons who inspired my interest in medicine as a young person. She said she and her husband had been very pleased I went into medicine.

I was unaware of her familial relationship to Biederman, yet for some unconscious reason I mentioned him and asked if she knew him. That question confounded her for a second as the relationship must have been common knowledge to others. I told her of my long interest in the artist and how much I would like to meet him. Cheerfully she said she was sure Mr. Biederman would be happy to meet me and she knew just the right person to introduce us, his daughter Anna who was on the premises. We searched for her but alas could not find her. Then Mrs. Hedin said a young resident sculptor, Max Cora, could make the connection as he saw Biederman almost daily.

So the search for Cora began. He was not in his studio. As we had a dinner engagement and time for our departure was rapidly approaching, I became apprehensive that the mission would miscarry. With just minutes to go we found him and Mrs. Hedin introduced us.

Max was a gentle person with a warm and ready smile. We liked him immediately. He told us he was accustomed to visit the artist around 5 PM to serve him his usual scotch cocktail he had enjoyed for many years. Usually he had two. On his next visit Max would ask Biederman about a visit from us and he would contact us in the next few days. Two days later I was thrilled to hear Max say on the phone our visit would be welcomed. I asked when. Why not tomorrow, Max replied.

Thus we planned to arrive for the 5 o'clock cocktail hour. With Max and Lucy in our VW Beetle we turned off the main highway onto a rutty gravel road. "There, up that driveway," Max instructed. The turn off was not readily apparent as it was obscured by a thatch of high wilted brown grass and bushes. Wheeling hard left we drove up an incline to arrive at a complex of buildings.

An old red barn stood on the left. To the right were two concrete block buildings, the artist's studios, appearing as though they had not been used for a long time. Further to the right stood three bright silver metal shafts jutting from beneath a heavy undergrowth of weeds and grass. Max said these sculptures reflected images and colors from the surrounding woods. Further to the right stood the wooden house dressed mostly in peeling white but also adorned in quadrants of the three primary colors. This was an artist's house. Here he had lived since the 1940's. (His wife died in 1976.) The house reminded me of my paternal grandparents'. Most likely it was constructed in the late 19th or early 20th century. The meager yard resembled a wild pasture.

None of the buildings or the grounds gave any sense of material wealth. In fact all looked penurious. One might have thought his success as an artist would have produced and attracted great wealth but there were no signs of it here. Having read of Biederman's independent nature and his uncompromising integrity the setting was entirely appropriate. Here was no conspicuous consumption. It fit the man's reputation completely.

Max ushered us through a small screened porch into the kitchen. There we were met by Karen, Biederman's care taker. She appeared to be in her 40's. After preparing supper and securing things for the night she would leave him alone except for his two cats.

From the kitchen we entered a large living room. On its walls hung a number of Biederman's works. There were abstract paintings from the 1930's together with the radiant three dimensional constructions characterizing his later years. In the same room was a modest cot where he slept. The next room was the office where Biederman sat awaiting us. Its two windows looked out on the road we had just traversed.

As Max introduced us as the great artist gripped our hands firmly. He commented on how firm Lucy's hand shake was. Because of cataracts and retinal disease his vision was impaired to the extent he had not worked for a number of years. It was an irony similar to that suffered by Monet. He looked at us with uncertain gaze but his voice was animated and his smile was warm. He seemed genuinely happy for our visit. We were awestruck to be sitting in private with such an icon of the arts.

As we circled our chairs Max poured each of us a ration of the Johnny Walker scotch I brought. Biederman was most congenial. He listened and laughed. There was no sign of arrogance or self importance. It was hard to believe. Max asked me if he could read one of my stories aloud: I nodded my assent with a good deal of apprehension grounded in the concerns I previously enumerated. Biederman liked the story. He said it was well-written and that of course pleased me immensely. Perhaps he was just being diplomatically charitable. Nonetheless, I accepted his compliment.

As the December afternoon light faded the artist arose to lower the window shades. Sipping our scotch we spoke of many things, I don't remember exactly what but it was all pleasant and interesting.

Shortly before 6 PM as dinner was ready for him, we said our goodbye. It had been a memorable heartwarming experience. On returning home I typed the name Charles Biederman on my computer web browser and came up with an astonishing 6000 citations. He was indeed famous.

Back to the question of cigars, Biederman said he had not returned to smoking. Max mischievously said the artist on occasion reflexively reached for the shirt pocket that previously held his cigars. I refrained from asking more questions on his decision but he volunteered, "No one makes you smoke." In other words, it was his choice and responsibility. It was an existentialist statement but he denied he was an existentialist.

A few days later I received a letter from him in which he again complimented me on another story I sent him concerning Michelangelo's statue of David. However, his comments on my piece about his cigar smoking were less laudatory. "Your essay on my quitting smoking, on the other hand, missed the mark. I made this decision myself, though it is true that my doctor got me thinking about it. Smoking was never a creative stimulus for me. What started as a simple pleasure became in the end a mere habit, and an unhealthy one at that. I realized that no one but myself was making me smoke, and that no one but myself could make me quit. After that it was simply a matter of stopping." I indeed had missed the mark. I had failed to consider the issue was one of simple self control that superseded considerations of health or creative stimulation. He was still in charge of his life. It was as simple as that.

He confirmed the story about butterflies hovering around him apparently attracted by his smoke but he said he didn't miss the cigars. About the same time he stopped smoking, his eye sight failed to an extent that prevented further creative work with his hands. Nonetheless, he did not stop his creative thinking. A 2002 publication testifies to a still active mind. No bitterness or irony was expressed as he talked about the loss of sight or other frailties attending age 96. Instead I sensed contentment over the body of creative work he had produced. He savored it as he did the scotch he sipped.

My opportunities to sit and sip scotch with world famous figures have been rare. When these moments occur, my sense of awe causes neglect of recalling details of conversation. Mainly, impressions remain of that afternoon, all positive.

In the days following, a fantasy came to me. I imagined a group of art critics and aficionados talking animatedly about Biederman's art. In a corner sits Biederman but no one pays attention to him. He is not offended as he quietly sits with a satisfied smile. The myth he has created has already transcended his physical person. The stature of an individual can often be measured by the stories and legends he or she inspires; witness those surrounding Lincoln, Washington or Churchill. About Biederman many stories will be written and legends created that will spread far beyond the restricted borders created by elitist self-conscious art critics. Mark my words.

January 2003

Post script: Biederman died in his home on December 26, 2004 at age 98.

PART SIX

Essays

Teamwork

To most people the word "teamwork" has a positive connotation. It calls forth notions of sacrifice for the common good, the effacement of personal gain and an ultimate triumph for cooperation. The effects of teamwork are amply recorded in the annals of sport and warfare as well as in virtually every field of human interaction. It is easy to understand how success of any enterprise is enhanced by coordinated and integrated efforts of individuals seeking a common goal.

As is the case with most idealistic concepts there is potential for corruption of the ideal. The ideal can be invoked to mask the real motives of sycophants. In this regard the idea of teamwork is particularly exploitable for those who would coerce rather than inspire cooperation. In order to test the genuineness of teamwork an analysis of the components of teamwork is useful.

First, every example of teamwork is motivated by a goal or purpose. In the sports domain, winning is the primary goal. Some would assert that for team sports, at least in non-professional spheres, the primary goals are character development through the demonstration of the value of cooperative effort. In other words, teamwork is invoked for its own sake as an instrument of maturation. However, after the lessons of teamwork have been learned it is gaining of a prize that seems most important.

A second feature of teamwork is volunteerism or freely given cooperation. Immediately one will question how, for example, an enlisted person in a combat infantry company has given his assent to participation in a mission. There are two possible interpretations. First, he may have volunteered, deliberately placing him in the role of accepting orders. This would fulfill the criterion of freely given cooperation. What of the conscript who has resisted military service? There is no volunteerism here. This is true and that person may not be a team player. Yet, history is replete with stories of heroism and selfless team efforts on the part of conscripts. In these instances volunteerism is based on the secondary acceptance of circumstances beyond their control but over which they can still exercise some degree of freedom of action. One can save a buddy or the entire company by a selfless, freely selected and freely performed action as for instance falling on a grenade. Ultimately, the quality of the individual contribution can be assessed by the degree of freedom exercised in the acceptance of the goals of the team. If one does not share the goals or values of the group it is probably best for that individual to dissociate from the group if possible.

Another characteristic of teamwork is the definition or assignment of specific tasks. The player should perform within the parameters defined for his specific role. Acting outside the role may cause problems and jeopardize the mission. Again, sports teams provide good examples. The defensive corner back on a football team performs best when he patrols his assigned area of the field and is not decoyed to another place. Some times such errors of performance can be repaired by another player quickly seeing it and filling in. However, for optimal performance, team players must adhere to their assignments.

A final determinative feature of teamwork is leadership, usually by an individual. The leader is responsible for the whole team and the results of teamwork. If leadership is poor quite likely the goals of the team will not be realized. It is the leader who ought to embody all the elements of teamwork, namely the goals or purposes, the idea of volunteerism and the ability to properly make and discharge assignments. He or she must lead in front, pulling the team ahead, not standing in the rear pushing. Often there is a hierarchy of leadership. The head coach of a football team is the primary overall leader but on the field it is the quarterback or defensive captain who are secondary leaders. The characteristics of leadership are the same. However, it falls to the primary leader to select the secondary leaders and define the goals of the team.

Teamwork can be corrupted by perturbations in any of the elements or characteristics discussed above. The goal may be ignoble as was the case with the Nazi movement. One of the chief "teams" in the movement was the SS, the elite military organization. In its early development the SS was constituted of predominantly volunteers who were fanatics for the Nazi cause. They were meticulously organized into specialized units for specific roles. In the early part of World War II the results of SS teamwork were notably successful. The quality of secondary leadership was high. Of course, Adolf Hitler was the primary leader or *Führer* as he was known. He used teamwork to define his friends as well as his enemies. Those who refused to play his game were marginalized, executed or forced to flee.

In less turbulent arenas the distortion of teamwork can have similar bad effects. Corporations, particularly in the 1990's, have frequently used teamwork to force cooperation and con- formity. Deviations from the corporate canon, even if minor and done with constructive intent, may have put the deviant at risk of reduced status if not dismissal. The stated goals of the corporation, as for instance "customer service above all", may simply be a disguise for activity with a less noble intent such as to make money in any way possible while employees are held in line by corporate slogans.

Another example of similar controlling efforts is to be found in the euphemistic advertisements for various health care plans. They espouse an overarching concern for patient care while delivering less than advertised in a suspected effort to simply generate profits. Such advertising is probably intended more to attract subscribers than to ensure the delivery of the highest quality of health care. The genuineness of published goals is difficult to test and rests on the motivations of the promulgators. Motivation can best be judged indirectly by examining the concordance of goals with results.

Thus, when "teamwork" is preached the discerning hearer will analyze the call on the basis of the nature of the stated or perceived goals, the roles participants play, the degree of volunteerism or freedom of action permitted and finally the quality of the leadership. When all the elements are deemed to be proper the results stand a high probability of success. When they are not, the potential players should beware.

The Nature of Work

I grew up with an ambiguous concept of work. This I attribute to the examples of my grandfathers. My maternal grandfather (hereafter designated as MGF) immigrated to the U.S. as a child of about two years. He and his parents and siblings came from the province of Smoland in southern Sweden where they had been farmers.

The concept of work developed by my grandfather is understood by firsthand knowledge of Smoland. Smoland is often referred to as "dark Smoland." It is covered with dense pine forest that shuts out sun light. Small plots of barely tillable land are irregularly dispersed throughout the brooding dark forests. The plots are usually surrounded by fences made of rocks cleared from the fields. The fields are laced with a residue of small stones. The earth is shallow. It is a wonder that any crops can grow.

The Swedish farmer usually rented his small plot or simply worked for the landowner. A portion of what little could be produced went to the owner as payment. What remained was often barely subsistence. At times the family was near starvation if the crops were poor. Thus, the crofter had to exert mightily for what little he had. Work was the constant activity that shut out thoughts of a dismal past and an unpromising future. It is quite understandable why large numbers of these poor farmers heard the siren call of the new world, America, and emigrated in the mid and late 19th century. They had nothing to lose.

Although MGF was just a toddler when he arrived in the new world and probably had little consciousness of the pathos in Smoland, the work ethic of his parents was quickly inculcated in the youngster. The homestead in Minnesota was immense and the soil deep and black. The habits of hard work learned in the old world would continue undiminished in the new. MGF was used to sweaty labor as a child. He could do nothing less up until he died at age 85. He expected the same of me.

Following the death of my grandmother at age 35, MGF was left with five children ranging in age from three to twelve years. My mother was second oldest but the oldest of the three girls. Responsibility for the household devolved on her at the age of nine. She too early learned the lesson of hard work. MGF was to spend his remaining years in uncompromising antipathy toward pleasure and comfort. The disaster of his wife's untimely death recalled from the depths of his sub-consciousness, the hard lessons of dark Smoland.

His idea of work as a hard continuous process fit the psychological armor guarding him against the cruel events confronting him. Work was his diversion from reality. Work was a part of reality he could control. This hard, depressive view of work was not uncommon to Swedish immigrants of the time. Perhaps it was a necessary faculty that enabled survival of the rigors of emigration. I was expected to assimilate the same lesson but I rebelled.

It was the more enticing lessons I learned from my paternal grandfather (here after called PGF) that saved me from a life of hard work. This grandfather had also emigrated from Sweden when he was just two. His temperament was quite different. He was full of joy and good times. The only concern he kept for tomorrow was his vision of my good fortune.

PGF came from a different background. He was the scion of the oldest nobility family in Sweden. His forebears had enjoyed power and wealth although this had been attenuated by the waning stature of the Swedish aristocracy in the 19th century. The reasons for emigration remain an enigma. The historical record, meager as it is, suggests that due to some malfeasance of his progenitors, PGF family fell on hard economic times; like MPG and his family the lure of a better life in America was irresistible. Eventually, they settled on a 40 acre farm in Wisconsin. The yield was marginal. The family grew to include eight children. There was too little money for education of the children except for that provided by the rudimentary primary schools of the time. In fact, PGF began working as a cattle herder at the age of 13. He subsequently worked as a railroad laborer and eventually learned the carpentry trade that sustained him and my grandmother until he retired. Church building became a preferred object of his trade. My grandmother used to say that her husband built the church but only she went to it.

PGF was always aware of his aristocratic background. It must have been a puzzling and depressing realization that this once proud and influential family had sunk so low on the social scale. Although his bearing was always distinguished, as he grew older he took little notice of his dress. He became a tattered, unkempt spectacle. Inside, the nobility remained as did his joy of life. When he worked he worked hard with sweat dripping from his brow. Physically he worked as hard as did MGF but there was a difference. He knew when to stop and enjoy himself. Work was not an obsession. It was a means to his pleasure.

Among his pleasures were tobacco and alcohol. He began smoking a pipe at age 13 and continued until his death at age 90. Friday nights were always special; then he would join his friends after work for a few drinks at a place called "The Barrel House." If we happened to be at the grandparental home Friday nights the anxiety level was quite high as we awaited PGF's arrival. My grandmother did not accept his drinking although she could not persuade this powerful man from any of his habits. He was by no means an alcoholic but on occasion he would have his surfeit. He would burst through the door surrounded by a plume of alcohol and smoke. These aromas have never left me. Today they still evoke his presence. He would pick me up and dance around the room while my grandmother apprehensively encouraged him to be careful. Their marriage would endure almost 70 years ending with their deaths a few months apart.

Thus, I was exposed to two polar views of work; the one characterized by hard, continuous, painful physical exertion that brought no joy; the other, was a means to provide the necessities of life that included leisure and play. To MGF, if what was called work was enjoyable it was not work. If it did not raise a sweat it was not legitimate. To PGF if work caused pain it should be minimized. Find some other kind of work that was enjoyable. In short, MGF's philosophy invalidated mind work whereas PGF affirmed it.

Even though I adopted PGF's philosophy, a remnant of the other persists. I still reflexly recoil from a colleague who complains of hard work as he sits in air-conditioned comfort, his only physical activity being the manipulation of a pen on paper; or another colleague may complain of hard work entailed in giving a few lectures on a subject of his expertise in an exotic venue. Although these examples may conjure a momentary ambivalence, I am firmly in the camp of PGF.

An examination of the physical definition of work may be illuminating to this discussion. Work equals force times the distance over which the force acts. Force has magnitude as well as direction. In this equation lets us substitute effort for force and time for distance. We can then say that work, in a social sense, is proportional to effort expended over a specified period of time. Since effort (force) has dimensions of magnitude and direction, we could then revise the definition of work to: work equals effort over a specific time period with purpose (direction).

In the context of this discussion, MGF would say the force is physical and PGF would say it is largely mental. Regarding the dimension of time, unceasing would be MGF's definition while PGF would say it should be intermittent and adjustable according to the situation. The most important dimension is direction for which I have substituted purpose. I'm really not sure why MGF worked. As I suggested earlier, his work ethic arose in a background of deprivation. Hard work was of necessity physical and constant. Even though deprivation ceased in America, the momentum of the ethic carried on long past its usefulness. In addition, MGF's early loss of spouse and the dependency of a large young family probably required some protective mental mechanism to shield him from the pain of the poverty of his emotional and spiritual loss.

The purpose of work for PGF was quite obvious. He may have been subjected to poverty in America but somehow there was an irrepressible capacity for joy and optimism that overcame any form of impediment to the affirmation of life and his hope for his posterity. One could make the case that his aristocratic lineage may have played a role in his outlook, whether due to genetic or environmental influences can not be said. I was exposed to two contrasting views of work. Perhaps it was the luck of my genetic endowment that governed my selection of the more congenial one.

The Fear of Rote

Many observers of primary and secondary American education agree there is need for reform. In spite of ostensibly modern and progressive educational theory and methodology introduced and applied over the past three decades, the system continues to deteriorate. Part of the problem, I feel, lies in the fear of rote memory.

A vocal faction of educators has declared that rote memory is to be discouraged as an archaic, boring method that does not engage the student and discourages enthusiasm for learning. It is a paradox that as respect for rote memory has declined so has the quality of education. Is the connection fortuitous or real?

The human brain may be compared to a computer. Before a computer can function it must be programmed with myriad bits of discrete data. Similarly, the brain must be programmed with basic information to enable higher cognitive processes. Some of the basic bits of data include numbers, simple mathematical tables, alphabet, grammar, historical places and dates to name a few. These are easily acquired by rote learning. Attempts are made to dress up this simple process with collateral associations as is done on the children's television program, Sesame Street. Whether this improves learning is open to question. What is most important is that the basic bits of data are imprinted on the brain at an early age when it is most receptive. If these bits of data are not available, there can be no basis for later complex thinking.

In high school my history teacher required her students to memorize what she called the "minimum essentials." These were summaries of the material presented during the previous week's classes. It was remarkable how well I and my fellow students performed. As the year progressed it became progressively easier as though the process of rote memory itself was being learned and honed. Not only were we learning facts, we were learning to use our memories. It is probable that our motivation stemmed as much from fear of failure as it did from the intrinsic interest of the subject. Nevertheless, we acquired a body of facts, i.e., bits of data that were firmly embedded in our brains. Perhaps there was more rigor than enjoyment but the job was done.

As I reflect on that history teacher I increasingly see the wisdom of her approach. As a student I considered her methods to be drudgery and herself an old fuddy duddy. However, no choice other than failure was open to me. She was totally unapologetic. Today she has my gratitude because she supplied the basis of my passion for history. Armed with her facts, acquired by rote, I have been able to absorb and critically evaluate history. Now that I have the basics I have ascended to a higher level of non-rigorous enjoyment of history. That is the order in which it should come. I was not injured by the original rigor. A similar lesson can be applied to any field of learning. Before one can perform higher mathematics the brain is programmed with simple addition, multiplication and division tables. Acquiring another language requires rote memory of alphabet, grammar and words if it is not learned within the culture of the language. Rote has a major influence in creating the foundation for what is to come.

It is difficult to say how the fear of rote came to be. Since it was a fundamental feature of older education it was probably proscribed simply because it was old. This conforms to a modern imperative of discarding all that is old regardless of its proven value. This seems like self destructive behavior.

What may play a more determinative role in the fear of rote is the current discomfort of imposing rigor on learning. There appears to be an overweening reluctance on the part of educators to impose stress or inconvenience, or a heightened sense of personal responsibility in the process of education.

If American primary and secondary education is to be rescued, rigor must be re-established. A part of this rigor is rote memory. It is not a part of some senescent doctrine. Rather, it conforms to relevant models of how the human brain is programmed for higher function.

The Fear of Ignorance,
the Joy of Knowledge

It is common for educators of young people to state that one of the most important goals of their efforts is to instill in their students intellectual curiosity. A body of information at any segment of time is mutable so that new information must be constantly assimilated if the individual is to maintain competence not only in work but in everyday life activities as well. At the end of formal education, it is the self-motivated, curious person who will be open to new information, to seek it out and critically evaluate it to maintain competence. Such a person is likely to ride with or above the waves of time and events to become a successful citizen. The unmotivated individual is likely to fall into intellectual poverty, disadvantaged not only economically and socially but spiritually as well.

Infants and children demonstrate a natural curiosity of their environment that biologically draws them out toward maturity. Once this constitutional curiosity dissipates it must be replaced by some other motivation to continue the exploration of an environment that now encompasses not only physical objects but the metaphysical world of ideas. Parents or their surrogates preside over infantile curiosity and then, in most circumstances, teachers become the chief custodians of education. That is not to say that parents are no longer important. They are exceedingly so but now the teacher shares the responsibility. The main task through the maturation process is how to seamlessly supplant original constitutional curiosity with a long term enduring intellectual curiosity through education.

Intellectual curiosity may be dissected into three major phases. We have already discussed the innate or constitutional curiosity of childhood. The next phase could be called utilitarian or vocational. In this phase the primary motivation is economic, to find a job with its implications of security, sustenance and shelter. Utilitarian curiosity may also involve the acquisition of information to maintain personal prestige. Utilitarian motivation can be very intense, perhaps in some people's lives, the most significant of them all. Sadly, it may end there not resolving into the highest form of curiosity, the ineffable and sublime.

In the state of ineffable sublime curiosity one seeks knowledge for its own sake unsullied by motivations previously described. A person imbued with ineffable-sublime curiosity continually explores the physical and metaphysical environment with unaffected desire and pleasure. No longer is knowledge sought for a purely economic reason. It is sought simply to satiate an esthetic impulse that when fulfilled leaves a sense of well being and self-respect. In this phase intellectual curiosity becomes a pure faculty with the potential of sustaining joy to the end of life.

The three phases of curiosity do not necessarily develop sequentially. Either by accident of circumstances or by deliberate intention a child can be enticed at an early age to acquire a utilitarian and an ineffable-sublime curiosity simultaneously.

A first requirement of educational strategy is to convince each pupil of their ignorance and poverty of knowledge. If properly done this should foster an abhorrence of ignorance or at least discomfort with it. In order to do this the individual must be given a view of how much there is to know and experience. This implies exposure to the breadth of human experience and categorical knowledge such as science, history, sociology, the whole gamut. So as not to be overwhelmed and frustrated by the magnitude of what there is to learn and experience, a sense of perspective should be instilled that says all knowledge cannot be embraced; the quest is the most important. Thus, much will be left to mystery and mystery in turn will further stimulate curiosity.

Travel is an important element in stimulating intellectual curiosity. Travel at once becomes the broad instructor exposing one to the whole gamut of human experience. It raises the individual out of a circumscribed environment and highlights both the differences and the similarities of mankind and increases awareness of new mysteries to explore. One is confronted with language that is not understood. It gives a sense of isolation from the culture, a disorientation that must be righted stimulating the learning of another language. Learning a language then opens another storehouse of knowledge creating more mysteries and enticing areas to explore; the whole process expands by geometric proportions. A fear of ignorance plays a role in this sequence to be sure. As rewards of intellectual curiosity accumulate, fear is replaced by joy and fulfillment.

While fear of ignorance is the predominant motivation it can be strengthened by periodic reminders of what one does not know. This can take the form of formal tests and other kinds of evaluation. Rewards of success should be extolled and respect for enlightenment and education cultivated. There is a carrot-stick dichotomy operative in the evolution toward ineffable-sublime curiosity.

Is it worth it? One can be a good citizen by just getting a job and providing for a family. To go beyond the utilitarian-economic motivation may be deemed unnecessary for most of the population. The haughty ineffable-sublime crowd must be strange and in a minority; maybe. I would suggest that attitude defines a major source of trouble with our educational system and its masters. It ought to be the goal of everyone to achieve ineffable-sublime curiosity to become oriented in this complex world; to become an even more effective citizen; to finally come to a state of utter fascination with being.

1610047

Made in the USA